From the author of *Culture Shock! Hawaii*

SO-AKT-176

Where

in the

World

Do I

Belong??

Belong??

BRENT MASSEY

Where in the World Do I Belong?? is for people who are looking to find themselves and other like-minded people. We are all different and there is no way one country fits everyone living in it. Many people who travel or live abroad are surprised to discover countries that fit them better than their own country. Discover if your personality type differs from your country's type.

The popularity of personality type theory is spreading throughout Europe, Asia and the rest of the world. Every year, millions of people take personality tests like the Myers-Briggs Type Indicator® (MBTI®). These people seek to understand themselves and others through the tool of personality type. *Where in the World Do I Belong*?? describes countries from around the world using personality type.

Insightful quotes and personal experiences of people from around the globe make *Where in the World Do I Belong*?? come alive. Cartoons by TRIGG illuminate and humorously depict various personality types and people from other cultures. *Where in the World Do I Belong*?? includes personality type profiles of more than 115 countries: Australia, Brazil, Canada, China, Finland, France, Germany, India, Iran, Iraq, Japan, Korea, Mexico, Nepal, Netherlands, Nigeria, Pacific Islands, Russia, Saudi Arabia, Spain, Sweden, Taiwan, Thailand, Tibet, Uganda, UK, USA, and more!

Find out what country you are for traveling and living abroad. *Where in the World Do I Belong*?? is also a tool for intercultural studies, cross-cultural trainers and anyone doing international business. *Where in the World Do I Belong*?? is a revolution in the way we understand ourselves and where we fit in the world.

WWW.BRENTMASSEY.COM or WWW.TYPEANDCULTURE.COM

SELF-HELP/TRAVEL

ISBN 0-9790397-0-3

51695

9 780979 039706

Where in the World Do I Belong??

BRENT MASSEY

Copyright © 2006 by Brent Massey

Published by Jetlag Press

All illustrations by TRIGG

All rights reserved

No portion of this book may be reproduced in any form or by any means without the written permission of the publisher.

The Step II Facet Scales on page 22 & 23 are modified and reproduced by special permission of the Publisher, CPP, Inc., Mountain View, CA 94043 from MBTI® Step II Manual. Copyright 2001 by Peter B. Myers and Katharine D. Myers. All rights reserved. Further reproduction is prohibited without the Publisher's written consent. Myers-Briggs Type Indicator, MBTI, Myers-Briggs, and Introduction to type are trademarks or registered trademarks of the Myers-Briggs Type Indicator Trust in the United States and other countries.

For information about special discounts for bulk purchases,
please contact brentmassey@brentmassey.com

––––––––––––––––––––––––––––

Library of Congress Cataloging-in-Publication Data
Massey, Brent.
        Where in the World Do I Belong?? / Brent Massey.
        p. cm.
        Includes index
        1. Self-actualization (Pychology). 2. Typology (Pychology). 3.
        Myers-Briggs Type Indicator. 4. Foreign Travel. 5. Intercultural
        Communication. 6. International Culture. I. Title.
        ISBN 0-9790397-0-3

Library of Congress Control Number: 2006935978

––––––––––––––––––––––––––––

Printed in the USA and UK

http://www.brentmassey.com

DEDICATION

This is dedicated to my wife,
Naoko Wada Massey,
who acquiesced to my folly of pursuing a dream.
To my children who shared their father with his work.
And to my readers,
who I hope to have served to the best of my ability.

ALSO BY BRENT MASSEY

Culture Shock! Hawai'i

Contents

The Next Level of the "Ah-Ha" Experience!

It's easy to see differences between people at work or in an intimate relationship but few people ever realize the differences between themselves and the culture they live in. Most people don't realize their personality type is different from the one their countries' culture rewards. Type and culture can be understood with the same personality type tools used for work and relationships.

You can't choose the family or the culture you were born into. We are stuck in these relationships for life. It's not like changing a job, getting a divorce, or even moving away. They will be with us until we die through mental programming and unresolved conflicts that we unconsciously replay wherever we go. We can only try to understand our differences.

Discover the personality types of your family members are and suddenly you understand why all those years there were misconceptions, misunderstandings, and unmet expectations. The same with your country's culture—it's another "Ah- Ha" experience. People say, "I knew my type but I didn't realize all this time my country's culture was telling me to be different than that. Wow! That's why I had some inner conflicts and why a few social expectations didn't make sense to me."

Type and culture are a new paradigm in self understanding and the next level of "Ah-Ha". Personality type experts Isabel Myers and

David Keirsey brought us the first level of understanding with type in relationships. Otto Kroeger and others brought the next level with type and work. Now with a new millennium, a new generation, and other countries in the world learning type, we raise the level of understanding of type and culture.

Growing up in a culture has more effect on you than your longest job or your longest relationship. To see your culture from a new vantage point can take your breath away. It's like the awakening of culture shock when living in another country, but it's your own country. It's shocking because every person grows up thinking his or her country's ideology is supreme. To see it from the outside in, you can feel like you've been deceived your whole life, especially if your type is very different from the one your country rewards.

Reasons For a Book on Type and Culture

People study psychology and personality type to resolve their own problems. My personality type is INFP, which is the exact opposite of my country's (USA) ESTJ type. I am in a cross-cultural marriage. My wife's country, Japan, is ISFJ—a very different personality type from mine. My wife's personality type is ESFJ—which is also very different from INFP. Right now I am living in a foreign culture—the state of Hawaii. Hawaii's culture type is ESFP and very different from the ESTJ country type of mainland USA. I have had many opportunities to learn to value other types and other country types.

I have a personal motivation to understand country types but also as an INFP I desire to express my personal values and ideals. My desire is to have people from all countries, especially Americans, value the differences of others and other countries. "NFs want to investigate the complexity of human interactions but their ultimate goal is to improve the human condition." (DiTiberio, *Writing and Personality*)

We can learn from the introverted feeling Asians how to socially interact harmoniously in groups to the benefit of everyone. We can learn from the extroverted feeling Europeans how to be concerned with the welfare of others in and outside our country. We can learn from extroverted sensing Latin Americans how to enjoy the moment and live life to the fullest.

1

The Spirit of this Book

In Hawaii, up until recently, TV reporters would describe a wanted criminal as Japanese, Filipino etc. This is amusing because it assumes that the people reporting the crime could tell the ethnicity of the criminal after only seeing them for a few seconds. Now they just say Asian, Caucasian, etc—which still perpetuates racism.

Hawaii and the mainland USA are opposite extremes. On the mainland USA we have gotten so politically correct you can't describe someone using race. In Hawaii many people describe others using race (especially with jokes). Neither one seems to work. On the mainland we don't talk about race and pretend ethnic differences don't exist even though people are coming in from different cultures. We avoid stereotypes but at the same time have no system for understanding differences.

Talking about racial difference is the taboo in US, so people are quick to pull out the politically-correct language and completely avoid anything that might be a stereotype. As a result, we have lost the ability to have a dialogue about cultural differences in the US. Not to mention that fact that most Americans lack interest in other cultures, so what they do know is usually only stereotypes.

"We tend to stereotype those who are most different from ourselves because we understand them less well—a rule that holds true for type differences as well as cultural, racial, etc. For example, extraverts may stereotypically project on to introverts the awkwardness they themselves would feel when stuck without having something to say or some action to be involved in. The comfort the introvert feels in reflection and silences may not occur to the extravert." (Lawrence, *People Types & Tiger Stripes*)

"In interpreting differences we should avoid the tendency to stereotype. Perception of differences is only the first step in the process of personal and collective growth to be followed by the understanding, the respect, the appreciation, and the integration of the perceived differences." (Casas, 1996 Psychological Type and Culture Conference)

From Differentiating to Respecting Differences to Appreciating Strengths

One Canadian living in New Zealand had some insight into racism in New Zealand after growing up in Canada. "New Zealanders see themselves as not being racist yet they still have many of the trappings of a racist society. Ethnicity is always an issue in everything, whether for good or bad, especially in politics and in the media, to a degree that you would never see in Canada. They recognize differences; yet have not risen above differentiating yet. For example, in the media, every time a criminal is arrested, if he is not white his race is automatically used as an adjective to describe him/her. Not helpful, yet they do not see that as a negative thing."

"I think the proudest moment in my life came one day when my 8-year-old son and I were discussing a bullying problem with the principal at his school. The principal asked my son whether the boy harassing him was European or Maori. My son just looked at him confused. He re-phrased the question...Was his skin white or brown? My son looked at him and said 'I don't know. He was just a boy'."

"I really believe though that to beat racism, it must be a coordinated education and media focus, and attention detail is important. It may seem a bit over the top or overly 'politically correct' at times, but it appears to be working in Canada."

We can ignore race (skin color) on a political level but we can't ignore that ethnic differences exist on a social level—especially between different cultures. We have to value differences (as opposed to using them as reasons to discriminate)—essentially going beyond ignoring, recognizing or tolerating differences to actually appreciating them, to cast cultural differences in the light of strengths instead of weaknesses.

"Cultural differences arise from differing histories and requirements for survival. Appreciating and enjoying the diversity in cultures can be incredibly enriching on a personal level and strengthening for a society as a whole. Learning about why the differences exist gives an added depth to the experience. But it needs to be experienced without bias. That is not easy to accomplish."

"Speaking as an outsider looking in, and forgive me if I speak too bluntly, but there appears to be a lot of cultural superiority in America. How often do we hear 'America is the best country in the world', and various spins on the theme? Obviously not every American suffers from cultural superiority, and most Americans I have met are wonderful people, but I do not believe over-zealous patriotism is healthy for any culture."

Even this questionable American trait can be could be portrayed as a strength: Americans have confidence in their intellectual theory of how the world should be like the USA. However, the more Americans understand the different strengths of other cultures the less biased we will be. Portraying differences as strengths is the first step in eliminating bias. If people are educated about those strengths they will have much more positive experience when they encounter them (e.g. at home, traveling abroad, living abroad and when experiencing culture shock).

Categories

The descriptions of national character, behavior and culture in the country profiles contain some of the author's own observations but the majority are based on observations of the people who grew up in those countries. Of course, there will always be individual differences and differing opinions to any generalization made. To be able to describe another culture, especially the psychological traits of a people, we cannot avoid using generalizations.

Personality type is a system of categorizing people by the mental processes they prefer to use. Categories also raise the eyebrows of the politically-correct watchdogs. They think putting people into categories is just another form of stereotyping. However, it is natural for us as humans to categorize people. As humans, we naturally desire a system to understand the world around us. Categorizing people is a system everyone uses whether they admit it or not. The point is to take the sting and negativity out of our categories and learn to appreciate the strengths and weaknesses of each category. Turn negative stereotypes into genuine understanding and respect.

Instead of avoiding the issue of differences that we as Americans automatically do, let us value the differences and seek to truly understand other ethnic groups from their points of view. Personality type theory is the best tool for this. The Myers-Briggs personality type

theory is based on the 'gifts differing' perspective. We all (as individuals and as ethnic groups) have different gifts to offer the world.

The Myers-Briggs descriptions have been worked on for many years to remove bias and stereotype. They will never be perfect but they are as close as it gets to categorizing people without disparaging one group over another. That is the spirit of this book. The purpose is to emulate the 'gifts differing' philosophy in making the categorization of countries and ethnic groups.

Differences

The 'gifts differing' principle is based on the biblical concept of "each giving according to his or her gifts." We can't ignore that differences exist. How we describe those differences (in positive or negative terms) and what we do with that knowledge is important. We can use it to the disadvantage of others (through manipulation or discrimination) or for better understanding.

It is frequently said, "People are just people and its best not to generalize." Yet, left to our own devices of trying to understand others leads to our own distorted misconceptions of other people and cultures. Instead we must educate people about the differences and learn to value them. When we study different personality types we begin to value them and understand them beyond surface impressions.

Some may use their knowledge of personality type to place people or cultures in boxes. Preconceived notions are the price we have to pay for greater understanding that empowers our communication and relations. Classifying differences doesn't mean that individuals fit in a box. Everyone is unique and type is only a foundation—or more like a starting point for conversation and communication of differences. If we avoid this discussion and ignore differences, we disempower anyone who doesn't fit the norm or average.

Not everyone strictly adheres to the cultural norm. They have their own personal backgrounds, like their family upbringing, that can affect whether they act in accordance with the cultural norm. Their personality type may be the exact opposite of the cultural type so they may act different. In essence we have to take every person

at face value despite type, race or whatever. Type and culture offer a basic of understanding of groups—not rules for conduct or communication.

As we come to understand other types and cultures, our fear of the unknown goes away and we begin to appreciate their strengths. It takes a lot of study, discussion and observations before we begin to really understand another type or culture deep enough to no longer have a fear of the unknown.

It is just like adjustment to culture shock. Everything 'they' do seems like bad intentions or racist actions until we begin to understand exactly the reason why they behave in that manner, and we begin to expect them to act that way. We feel empowered because people from other cultures act like we expect them to act. We no longer project negative thoughts like racism on them.

2

Type Basics

Introverts concern themselves with their inner world of thoughts and feelings. Extraverts focus on the outer world—everything in the environment around them. People perceive their outer and inner environment through either sensing or intuition. They also have a preference to make decisions in either a thinking or feeling way. Everyone uses all of these perceiving and judging functions but we all have a favorite that we use more often.

Intuitive types will build staircases of thought out of clouds of abstract ideas and theories, but the sensing types need staircases built out of concrete facts and evidence—something they know will support them. Feeling types base decisions on personal and social values while thinking types rely on the logic of their intellectual conclusions.

Perceiving types will talk all day about their perceptions (the data they take in or inner reflections) through their observations, insights, ideas, comments etc. They are opening up the conversation for more input, different points of view etc. When listening to judging types you will hear them making judgments, decisions, voicing opinions, and driving towards closure. My wife says talking to me is like waiting for a punch line that never comes. As a perceiving type I will talk about something in depth but won't voice many

judgments. This is the classic communication difference between perceiving and judging types.

Function and Temperament Theory

Each letter combination produces different behaviors, interests, and values. Both Myers (*Gifts Differing*) and Keirsey (*Please Understand Me II*) found different pairs to be significant. Myers determined the main 'functions' as SF, ST, NF, and NT, whereas Keirsey determined the main 'temperaments' as SJ, SP, NF, and NT.

However, psychology professor Bernie Ostrowski believes we need to equally explore all the possible pair combinations. "When you look at significant pair results, in 49 Type Tables from 24 issues of the Journal for Psychological Type, you see significant results for all the of the 24 preference pairs, not just the ones singled out by the various theories."

Now, there are the MBTI Step II facet scales, which add another level of complexity and refinement. For each MBTI dichotomy there are five individual facets (at the end of this chapter is a list of the Step II facet scales). The Step II facet scales create an even greater level of accuracy by determining which facets of each dichotomy are preferred. The facet scales are an incredible tool because they can clarify differences between people of the same type. For example, two people can both be feeling types but one can have an 'out-of-preference' for being logical.

Type Dynamics

In addition to type pairs and facets there are type dynamics. Everyone has one favorite mental process and a second that acts as a helper.

This is how you can easily determine your favorite mental process: The second letter of your type is your perceiving function (intuition or sensing) and the third letter is your judging function (feeling or thinking). If you are an ISFJ you perceive the world with sensing and judge it with feeling. Judging and perceiving are always used in the opposite direction. For example, if you use perceiving in the outside world (extraverted) then you use judging in the inner world (introverted) and vice versa.

The last letter of your type tells you what you use in the outside world and the first letter of your type tells you where your favorite process is. An ISFJ has a 'J' at the end so that means they use their judging function in the outside world—they extravert their feeling. The first letter of ISFJ is 'I' which means their favorite process is in the inner world (introverted). Their feeling is extraverted so their sensing must be introverted, therefore introverted sensing is their favorite mental process. The remaining mental process, extraverted feeling acts as a helper in service to the favorite.

There are eight mental processes:

Perceiving
Extraverted Sensing
Introverted Sensing
Extraverted Intuition
Introverted Intuition

Judging
Extraverted Feeling
Introverted Feeling
Extraverted Thinking
Introverted Thinking

We all use the eight mental processes but each type has a different hierarchy of use. ESTJs prefers to use extroverted thinking. Their second preference is introverted sensing, and then their third preference is extroverted intuition, and so on. The ISFP prefers to use introverted feeling. Their second preference is extroverted sensing, and their third preference is introverted intuition, and so on.

Basically the mental processes equal three of the type letters. For example introverted feeling is the same as IFP. Add the second mental process of extroverted intuition and you have INFP. From this we can also tell the third and the fourth process. The third is the opposite pole (e.g. the N-S dichotomy) and world (inner or outer world E-I) of the second, therefore extroverted intuition is second and introverted sensing is the third. The fourth is also the opposite pole and world of the first. For example, introverted feeling is the first and extroverted thinking is the fourth.

As we grow older we develop ability with mental processes further down the hierarchy. The first process is developed as a child, the second as a teen, the third in our 20s-30s, and the fourth around mid-life.

Type experts are in disagreement over whether the third mental process is extroverted or introverted. Looking at my own type development, the third mental process apprears to be extroverted. I started developing my extroverted sensing (my third mental process) with my interest in playing the guitar and doing yard-work from about eighteen years old.

Personality Tests

If you don't know your personality type (e.g. INFP, ESTJ, etc.) and you want a quick indication of your type look at the Step II facet scales at the end of this chapter. Select the facets that fit you— the ones you prefer the most. Force yourself to choose between one of two opposite facets (e.g. initiating or receiving). The side you choose three or more facets is your preference (e.g. extraverted or introverted).

Also, it may be helpful to take one of the personality type tests. You can take a free online test based on the Carl Jung typology at www.humanmetrics.com or the test included in David Keirsey's book *Please Understand Me II*. The Keirsey Temperament Sorter test is also available online at www.keirsey.com. On the Keirsey website you can also take the test in sixteen different languages. There is a fee for the English version but foreign languages are free.

If you find your results aren't clear and want the most accurate test available check out the Myers-Briggs Type Indicator® (MBTI®). In the USA about three million people take the MBTI test each year. Isabel Myers created the MBTI. Her book *Gifts Differing* explains the MBTI but doesn't include the MBTI test. You can pay US$150 to take the test online at www.capt.org or by calling 800.777.2278. You can also pay to have a certified consultant administer the MBTI to you. Check out the www.mbticertification.org website for a list of consultants near you.

I recommend taking the MBTI if your results aren't clear (i.e. you are balanced/borderline on some of your preferences). For example, you're split evenly between preferring feeling or thinking. If you take the Step II test you will get even more clarification on your type preferences. If your native language isn't English check to see if there is a translation of the test—this will give you more accurate results.

All of these tests will give you a four-letter code (e.g. ENFP, ISTJ, ESFJ, etc.) These are based on the opposites of extraversion-introversion, sensing-intuition, thinking-feeling, and judging-perceiving.

The Spread of the MBTI in the World

There are many countries where you can take the test in your own language and also can read about personality type in translated versions of the popular books from authors like Myers, Keirsey, Kroeger and others.

The Myers-Briggs organization reports the MBTI has been translated into 20 languages. Browsing through the CAPT bibliography online there is a French MBTI translation in 1990, German in 1991, Swedish in 1992, Korean in 1992, and Japanese in 2000 (although they had an older translation in 1968). Also, 2004 was a big year for Dutch translations of the standard MBTI books.

The distributor of the MBTI test (Consulting Psychologist Press) has MBTI translations in Danish, Dutch, Finnish, French, Canadian French, German, Italian, Norwegian, Spanish, Argentinian Spanish, Swedish, European English, Portuguese, Australian English, Cantonese and Mandarin Chinese, Bahasa Malay, Korean, and Greek.

The Keirsey Temperament Sorter has been translated into fifteen languages: Spanish, Portuguese, German, Norwegian, Swedish, Bosnian, Polish, Czech, Danish, French, Russian, Finnish, Ukrainian, Chinese, and Japanese.

Step II Facet Scales
INTROVERSION (I)
Directing energy toward the inner world of experience and ideas.
- Receiving—reserved, low key, are introduced
- Contained—controlled, harder to know, private
- Intimate—seek intimacy, one-to-one, find individuals
- Reflective—onlooker, prefer space, read and write
- Quiet—calm, enjoy solitude, seek background

INTUITION (N)
Focusing on perceiving patterns and interrelationships.
- Abstract—figurative, symbolic, intangible
- Imaginative—resourceful, inventive, seek novelty
- Conceptual—scholarly, idea-oriented, intellectual
- Theoretical—seek patterns, hypothetical, trust theories
- Original—unconventional, different, new and unusual

FEELING (F)
Basing conclusions on personal or social values with a focus on harmony.
- Empathic—personal, seek understanding, central values
- Compassionate—tactful, sympathetic, loyal
- Accommodating—approving, agreeable, want harmony
- Accepting—tolerant, trusting, give praise
- Tender—gentle, tender-hearted, means-oriented

PERCEIVING (P)
Preferring flexibility and spontaneity.
- Casual—relaxed, easygoing, welcome diversions
- Open-ended—present-focused, go with the flow, make flexible plans
- Pressure-prompted—motivated by pressure, bursts and spurts, early starting is unstimulating
- Spontaneous—want variety, enjoy the unexpected, procedures hinder
- Emergent—plunge in, strategies emerge, adaptable

EXTRAVERSION (E)

Directing energy toward the outer world of people and objects.
- Initiating—sociable, congenial, introduce people
- Expressive—demonstrative, easier to know, self-revealing
- Gregarious—seek popularity, broad circle, join groups
- Active—interact, want contact, listen and speak
- Enthusiastic—lively, energetic, seek spotlight

SENSING (S)

Focusing on what can be perceived by the five senses.
- Concrete—exact facts, literal, tangible
- Realistic—sensible, matter-of-fact, seek efficiency
- Practical—pragmatic, results-oriented, applied
- Experiential—hands-on, empirical, trust experience
- Traditional—conventional, customary, tried-and-true

THINKING (T)

Basing conclusions on logical analysis with a focus on objectivity.
- Logical—impersonal, seek impartiality, objective analysis
- Reasonable—trustful, cause-and-effect, apply principles
- Questioning—precise, challenging, want discussion
- Critical—skeptical, want proof, critique
- Tough—firm, tough-minded, ends-oriented

JUDGING (J)

Preferring decisiveness and closure.
- Systematic—orderly, structured, dislike diversions
- Planful—future focused, advance planner, make firm plans
- Early starting—motivated by self-discipline, steady progress, late start stressful
- Scheduled—want routine, makes lists, procedures help
- Methodical—plan specific tasks, note subtasks, organized

Source: Quenk, Hammer, and Majors, 2001. Used with permission.

3

Functions/Mental Processes

I am a clear INFP with a strong preference on all the scales but I was still way out of touch with myself in regards to work that fit my type. I worked in sales after college and then IT for seven years. I was so imbalanced in my type that instead of verifying my type through the description, it was more a matter of using the type description as a manual of how to be my type. As I did the things described as typical traits of my type I actually felt more comfortable and balanced. Some were obvious like not answering the phone and letting it go to the answering machine. Others were subtler like realizing as an introvert I don't have to have an immediate answer to a question. I can give myself the liberty of taking my time to let it work its way through my brain before coming back with an answer. According to psychology professor Bernie Ostrowski, introverts take longer to respond because when they process something (like a question) it takes a longer path through the brain than an extravert. This is the reason for the pause in conversations and the introvert being comfortable with pauses.

DiTiberio's book on *Writing and Personality* clarified my strengths and weaknesses as an INFP writer. Some of my strengths as a writer were areas I may have discounted or avoided. For example, as an INFP feeling type my strength lies in writing in a personal way instead of impersonal and objective. Growing up in American culture I learned to discount my personal views and values for an impersonal and objective approach.

Further, as an intuitive perceiving type, I need to set limits on my research and digressions, otherwise I will keep gathering new data and never reach the closure needed to finish my book project. Sentence mechanics and grammar are a natural ability for sensing types, so as an intuitive type I don't let myself get obsessed with my weak spot, instead I keep it in mind as an area I need to develop my skills. Also, it is the same with building my vocabulary—what comes natural to a thinking type will take a little more work on my part as a feeling type. I work on improving my grammar and vocabulary but realize that those are sensing and thinking activities. So as an INFP I don't set my expectations too high for those activities (which can happen because we INFPs tend to be obsessed with perfection sometimes).

The most amazing realization, however, was how much I was out of touch with my type. When I allowed myself to live my type description I found peace, centeredness and clarity in my calling. I was so off center from growing up in ESTJ American culture and having weak boundaries (as many INFP do), that I got overrun by both American culture and my family, and lost my sense of who I was in the process. One INFP psychology professor believes INFPs need to understand their own unique personal mission, articulate it and set it into action.

Lastly, all types have different paths to becoming balanced. Australian type expert Peter Geyer said it is no use telling an INTP he needs to get in touch with his feelings. The problem is that when he is in touch with his feelings, he is operating in his inferior function, which causes stress, is rigid and produces poor results. As an INTP needs to understand his feelings through an intuitive-thinking route instead. Have it explained to him in an intuitive-thinking manner and allow him to process his experience in an intuitive-thinking way. For example, use logic and a systematic, objective approach to process feelings that surface when dealing with something like a divorce or culture shock (the reactions, anger, and other emotions one feels when coping with the differences in a new culture).

Each of the Eight Processes Has a Mission

When I'm writing a book I have to remind myself that my mission is an introverted feeling one, otherwise I will spend time writing things that I'm just not naturally good at. My mission isn't an extraverted intuitive one of having a better idea or argument than others; or an introverted intuitive one where I have ideas about the future. It is not an introverted thinking mission of naming and classifying the world or extraverted thinking mission of objective, logical, empirical research. Mine is not even an extraverted feeling mission to help people. No, it's an introverted feeling mission to improve the human condition. In my case it's to right the injustices done to people and societies around the world.

The mission of each mental process in a nutshell:

Introverted feeling: mission for humanity

Extraverted feeling: service to others

Extraverted intuition: grand play at ideas

Introverted intuition: confident predictions of future outcomes

Extraverted thinking: desire to manage the world

Introverted thinking: classifying and naming parts of systems

Extroverted sensing: desire to live in the moment and better than their rival

Introverted sensing: desire to live better than their experience and live up to the ideal.

Processing

My wife and I like to attend ethnic festivals. As an extraverted intuitive type, I enjoy a new experience, new faces and places, new undiscovered ways of seeing the world, and learning different ways people do things. As an introverted sensing type my wife enjoys a quality experience (sensory appealing, clean, new things) or a sensual one like tasty festival foods. At a festival she also enjoys nostalgic experiences, where she can recall pleasurable memories from the atmosphere, clothing, food etc. A little bit of sensual or nostalgic experience at a festival and that's all she needs and is ready to go home.

My wife and her sister are both introverted sensing types. They go to the beach or a festival and it only takes a little while before they are ready to go home and process what they have experienced. The pleasure is in the reliving, replaying, rehashing; going home and discussing the experience, the scenery, water, beach, foods, etc.

For introverted sensing types the internal processing of the experience is where the real pleasure is, as well as reliving it through discussion. It doesn't have to be reliving an experience that was in the distant past. It can be an hour ago. They can have an experience then go home and immediately start reliving it by talking about it. Discussion aids in defining and filing the memory experiences in their brains. An hour after coming home my wife is able to tell me how much she enjoyed the meat stick at the festival. She has already processed that part and deemed it enjoyable and memorable. By sharing this thought she is already reliving the experience—and it just happened a couple hours before!

For me as an introverted feeling type, I come home and process the people interactions I had during the festival. I take a little quiet, private time to process my feeling experiences internally. At the festival I prefer to stay longer and want to stretch the good feeling times for all their worth because I don't have the photographic memory an introverted sensing type does.

Introverted feeling is based on personal internal values. One of my personal inner values is the importance of my family. When I'm sitting on a lounge chair at Ko'olina beach and my children are running around in the sand and water, and the sun is in the late afternoon sky, I know this is as good as it gets. This is one of those special memory times—it resonates with my introverted feeling value of family—and I want it to last so I can recall the good feeling of seeing my children playing on a beautiful beach in their younger years. Yet, I too can have introverted sensing thoughts and remember the times I played on the beach with my brothers in California.

Memory

The memory of a sensing type is like making a photo of the experience; intuitive types are writing to memory and attaching symbolism to the experience; thinking types are making a record or log of the experience; and feeling types have a memory colored by their mood.

For example, when you combine the favorite (dominant function) with the helper (the second/auxiliary function) it might look like something like this: an ESFJ (feeling plus sensing) would have a personalized photo album and an INFP (feeling plus intuition) a written account in a personal journal (which, with the right wording can be as vivid as a photo album).

The ESFJ comes home and files the mental photos into drawers for later or if she has time she will edit her mental photo album, adding the pictures and putting captions to them. If her sister says she saw a turtle at the beach she will in essence take an image of a turtle off the Internet and paste a small one in her mental photo album as a reminder that the North Shore has a turtle beach. On the other hand, an extraverted sensing type might not pile up the photos but instead their memory would be like a digital camera that writes over any photos older than an hour.

For the INFP to write about an experience to memory is like a writer that immerses himself for a period of time and waits for things to rise to the surface of his mind through his muse—deeper insights, meanings and symbols. The journal entry or story in his mind becomes more symbolic with time.

Lastly, an introverted intuitive may not even notice the moment or may have an abstract memory like a pink beach.

Triggers

For all types an outside stimulus can sometimes trigger their preferred mental process. For the introverted sensor, an outside stimulus can start with the extraverted sensing experience, then switch to introverted sensing with the inner mental associations that it has set off. For example, when eating candy the crunch and taste is extraverted sensing but the associations to past candy experiences are the introverted sensing at work.

The mental images produced by introverted intuition can also be provoked by an extraverted sensing experience. These inner world images may then be distorted like an abstract painting and set off visions of other abstract images.

For extraverts the process stays in their outer world. The extraverted intuitive continues to gather more outside ideas (stimulus) for more connections and possibilities. The extraverted sensor also keeps in the outside world, but looks for more sensory experiences (visual, hands-on, etc.) instead of ideas.

Introverts

Introverts live mainly in the inner world and extraverts live mainly in the outer world. One introverts its dominant function and the other one extraverts it. Therefore, to operate in the opposite world (inner vs outer) of your dominant function takes more energy because you are using an inferior function that isn't developed or is immature. Many type experts give the example of using your left hand if you're right handed. It is difficult to write with your opposite hand and just like trying to use your opposite type. Using your opposite type all day would take a lot of energy and surely you would start slipping and making mistakes before the day was out.

Introverts need down time to be alone and reflect. As an introverted feeling type sometimes I don't know my real feelings, values or beliefs about a situation until I have had a chance to be alone and reflect on it. Then later, I may come back to a person and state my position or opinion.

Insight is used as a descriptor for introverted intuition. The Oxford American dictionary defines insight as "the capacity to gain an accurate and deep intuitive understanding of a person or thing." This definition fits introverted intuition but it also defines insight as "inner sight, mental vision, wisdom." All introverted processes have the gift of inner sight and mental vision through the inner world. My introverted feeling has insights about humanitarian issues, for example, I believe all types should be rewarded equally in society. Introverted sensing types have insights into the subtle differences between the present and the past. The introverted thinking person has insight into what something really is and the ability to name something for what it really is.

Introverts trust their inner process. Introverted sensing has associations with the past and introverted intuition has visions of the future. This is how they both perceive and interpret the world. Introverted feeling and introverted thinking have inner guides—the former for good and evil, and the latter for logic or illogic. This guide is used by their internal judging process to make decisions.

Introverted Functions

The extroverted functions are easy to see in action but the hidden subtleties of the introverted functions needs some explanation. The introverted perceiving and judging mental processes are grounded in the inner world of each person.

They say inspiration is part divine guidance. It may be that all introverted processes tap into this guidance in some form. Some might call it the soul and others like Jung call it the collective unconscious.

We envy the introverted feeling type's ability to see inside others, the introverted intuitive type's ability to see future ideas that no one else can, the introverted thinking type's ability to see inside a system, and the introverted sensing type's ability to remember and compare.

The introverted sensing type records all these sensory events and associations to past experiences but sometimes gets a reaction or response later through introspection when reviewing and filing. They can also fully relive a past experience or sensation. My wife smelled burning incense at a Christian church service, but there was no incense. The mesmerizing sermon of the minister and the women fanning themselves triggered a past association of the Buddhist temple services she attended as a child where incense was always burned during the service.

The mental images of the introverted intuitive are like flash-paper. A magician uses flash-paper for special effects. The paper is lit and quickly consumes itself with a flash and leaves nothing behind. An introverted intuitive type sometimes can't explain or articulate how the mental image came about or even how it relates to the here and now. They try to communicate this image flash before it vaporizes or morphs into something else.

Introverted feeling is colors and tones radiating out like a constantly changing kaleidoscope. I have these unexplainable feeling tones about other people telling me whether that person is up to no good or not. I can't explain why I know this but it comes to me in feeling tones and somehow I know a person's intentions within the first meeting.

The immediate feeling impression I get off someone is so complex that it would take a great deal of analysis before I might even understand the origin of it. But that is an attempt to give logic to a subjective process, which is a worthless task in itself. The subjective mind must be trusted just as much as objective logic—especially when it can't be explained logically. The subjective must be explained with subjective tools: universal truths, inner beliefs, and personal values. These are the colors that make the kaleidoscope of feeling tones and shades. For an introverted feeling type, every movement among people is like walking through a moving kaleidoscope. Sometimes shades of red on one side; sometimes cool blues on another side. Emotions are the esthetic reactions to the mosaics viewed in the kaleidoscope.

The introverted thinking type has a cascade of logical linkages, like a tree diagram of clusters of information or like a relational database with multiple links between multiple thoughts. When they encounter people and situations it's like running a query against their inner relational database. Do their classifications and categories consistently work against the world they experience? If not, they must add those database entries or at worst, have to restructure and redefine until is does.

A thinking type tries to find inconsistencies in ideas and a feeling type finds the flaws in value systems of individuals or societies. Introverted thinking people can see principle flaws in a system and introverted feeling people can feel ethical failings in a person. Introverted thinking types can give you an overall judgment of a complex system whether it will work or not, whereas introverted feeling types can give you a judgment on the overall essence of a person or group situation. For example, thinking types can be great with technical systems and feeling types can be great at hiring people.

Balance

My favorite mental process is introverted feeling so I need to make judgments and decisions during private time. However, I get my data or perceptions from my extraverted intuition so I need to look to others in the outside world for information. Talking with others is like a breath of fresh air when I am trying to figure out new ideas or stuck on a problem. I get my best information from other people, which is why I enjoyed learning about other countries' types through listening to what people said about their countries. I've found that I don't have to always do it face to face either and email works just as well. But I must be careful and not spend too much time in the outer world with my extroverted intuition because "IPs who do not protect their introverted time starve their dominant function" (Brownsword, *It Takes All Types*).

Once I have the information I need, I sit at my desk (by myself) and make judgments about that information. My inner compass (to universal truth) guides my decisions and tells me if I am barking up

the right tree and whether I am headed in the right direction with my writing and in my search for information.

My third (extroverted sensing) and fourth (extroverted thinking) mental processes are immature and inferior compared to my favorite process, introverted feeling, or even my second preference that is extroverted intuition. I get in over my head on thinking conversations when my extroverted thinking gets overused and starts slipping like a worn -out car transmission. I start blabbing things I didn't want to say because I'm trying to keep up with a technical thinking conversation and soon start slipping, especially if I am already tired or already used up my thinking quota for the day. This also happens when I'm doing handyman projects (using extroverted sensing) at home and soon start to get muddled in the head, confused, and can't remember what step I was on in the instructions and start making poor decisions on how and what to do.

The solution is to step back into my favorite (dominant) process by guiding the thinking conversation into a feeling direction. Sometimes the thinking types listen with red faces and then go back to their thinking track conversation and at that point I have to let go and stop trying to keep up. The same with my handyman projects, I save it for the next day when I have a fresh quota of sensing and thinking at my disposal.

As an introvert, in the outer world, dealing with people, I will always be using my inferior processes so I don't try to appear to be better than the process. I allow myself to be an introvert and when asked a question take a second to let it flow through my brain and I don't have to make a joke or fill the dead air spaces. Also, I try to get out of my head and into my heart. If I need to make a decision, I should rely on my inner feeling process. I feel more balanced and secure not trying to understand thinking type research or conversations all the time. The answer can be as simple as reading INFP authors instead of INTJ research papers.

I recognize the signs of when I am slipping into my dark side and that means I must step back. I don't try to fix where I already slipped up because this just makes me more stressed and keeps me in the inferior process longer. If it's a social situation, afterwards I come home and regain my balance by chilling out in my room, reading a book or something. The third function is used as a source of levity. According to one type expert, when you find yourself slipping into your dark side try using your third mental process to regain balance. My third process is sensing, so I go pull weeds in the yard.

The mental processes are also subtle signals of imbalance in your life. When someone tunnels too deeply into their preferred process, they can develop tunnel vision. For example, types that have judging function as their favorite (EJ, IP) can be blind to new facts, new ideas and at the extreme, be one-track and close minded, rigid and judgmental. Types that have a perceiving function as their favorite (EP, IJ) may have poorly defined values and principles and at the extreme, flaky with no ethics. Therefore, you must develop your second function because it creates balance between these extremes.

4

The Power of Type

Type isn't just a set of traits or a list of adjectives—it's an indicator of a bigger picture. The four letter type code indicates which of the eight mental processes/functions is our favorite. This favorite is the sole driving force in a person or culture. Forget about lists of traits and behaviors and just learn how each mental process functions. This is the way to truly understand the mind of a person or a culture.

Our mental processes are biologically hardwired in our brain. We use our favorite function in either the public outer world or the private inner world. The inner world draws on principles and values, past and future experiences. The outer world draws on societies expectations, laws, the here and now, and infinite possibilities.

Our favorite mental process/function is partly unconscious. That is why you may find people, foods, languages, religions that somehow click with your own mental process partly on a subconscious/unconscious level. This is the kind of connection or experience that gives you joy and peace but you don't know why. It's too deeply psychological and spiritual to explain. It's like following your personal calling. You don't usually know the destination but for some reason you know you are headed in the right direction and it gives you joy and peace.

Similarity

In the following chapters I have arranged and paired the personality types based on the favorite function—type experts call this the 'dominant mental process' or 'dominant function'. It is easier to understand each of the eight dominant mental processes if they paired together. For example, the dominant function of ISFJ and ISTJ is introverted sensing. The secondary functions (e.g. the secondary function of ISFJ is feeling and ISTJ is thinking) are like an added modification on the dominant function. Organizing the types this way helps you understand what introverted sensing would look like alone and when you add the secondary functions of thinking or feeling.

On the other hand, these pairings don't necessarily represent the closest or most similar type. The extravert and introvert pairings are also very similar. For example, INFP and ENFP both prefer intuition and feeling but for INFP feeling is dominant and for ENFP intuition is dominant. There are similarities in an E-I pairings in addition to the dominant function pairings like ISFJ and ISTJ.

Under each type chapter are a lists of countries grouped by regions (Asia, Africa, etc). The regions and countries are not listed alphabetically but instead organized according to similarity, regional proximity and which countries struck me as particularly clear examples of type.

Each chapter includes all of the countries that fit that particular personality type (i.e. ISTP, ENFJ, etc.). The countries in each chapter share similiar preference for one mental process. Therefore, similar patterns of behavior can also been seen.

All of the quotes in the country profiles are from people who were born and raise in that country. I interviewed dozens of international students at the University of Hawaii and exchanged email correspondence with hundreds of people from more than 115 countries around the world. There were over 400 people who commented on their countries so the quotes have not been attributed.

The following table is a graphic representation the type of each country. The left side of the table is Introversion, iNtuition,

Feeling, and Perceiving. The right side is Extroversion, Sensing, Thinking, and Judging. The gray bars extend from the middle out to the sides. In this sample country, Utopians prefers extroversion clearly over introversion, whereas they only prefer intuition slightly over sensing.

Utopia is ENFJ:

Clear				Slight			Clear
I				▓	▓	▓	E
N			▓				S
F			▓				T
P				▓			J

Under each table is a list of facets that are out-of-preference. For example, concrete (S), traditional (S), reasonable (T), and critical (T). The end of Chapter 2 has a decription of each facet. These facets are exceptions to the overall type preference. For example, Utopian culture is an intuitive type but also prefers the facets of concrete and traditional—which are part of the opposite preference of sensing.

Cross-Type Communication

My wife and I have sensing and intuitive conversations that are examples of superior functions talking to inferior functions. I find her common sense not exactly 'common' for me because I am listening to a superior function (sensing is my third function and is her second). The same for our intuitive conversations, she tosses out an idea (intuition is her third function and my second) and I tend to discount it as a 'common idea'—something I already know, or we have discussed before but it's her extraverted, chatty side that wants to 'review'. She looks at me like I have no common sense and I look at her like her ideas are all common!

Similar types understand each other without a lot of explanation. My wife likes to make amusing comments to people who can get it—people who have shared a common experience with her. My ESFJ wife and her ISFJ sister are like this—much more so than I am with my brothers, or even more than between her and her mother.

I speculate it is because their types are similar. My wife wrapped washcloths around frozen ice-pops for the kids to hold while eating them. Her sister said, "you're going to use those washcloths for the children's bath after this aren't you?" They laughed because they know each other so well and they had a common understanding through having similar mental processes. This is also the introverted Japanese culture where people tend to understand your intentions without explanation.

Unconscious Motivation and Desire

As an American I grew up loving Mexican food. Mexico is ESFP and I am INFP so we have FP in common. I discovered Indian food later in life and love it as much as Mexican food. India is ENFP and I am INFP, so we have NFP in common. I imagine that if I had grown up with both Indian and Mexican food I would love Indian food a bit more. It's a subconscious thing—you resonate with a similar country type's food. It's the same with advertising. Suddenly I found advertisements in other countries that were much more appealing, not because they were new, but because they are closer to my type. Advertisements were more appealing to me than American ones because ESTJ American culture is the opposite of my own INFP type.

The US Foreign Service classifies foreign languages by difficulty for an English speaker to learn. Japanese is classified as the hardest, Thai as moderate and German as easy. I studied Japanese, Thai, and German and found Thai was more pleasing to my ear and soothing to my brain. Thai was much more enjoyable to learn than Japanese or German. I have two preferences in common with ESFP Thai culture, only one with ISFJ Japanese culture, and none with ISTJ German culture.

Language is the vehicle of culture and is both a conscious and unconscious subtle programming that teaches us culture. For example, we learn what is important in a culture by what words that are left out or used more often or if there are several words for one meaning. Even taboo words tell us about culture type. It is easier to study a language from a country similar to your type because the language is programming built for your type.

My attraction to Asia was an introverted feeling one. Thailand, Burma, Cambodia, India, Nepal, and China all have introverted feeling as their first or second preference; and Japan, Taiwan and Korea have extraverted feeling as their first or second preference. I am an INFP and I married into an ISFJ culture (Japan). ISFJ is very different from my type but still a feeling culture, which is closer to my introverted feeling type than American extraverted thinking culture.

There are multiple possibilities for psychological attraction beyond a country's food, language or love interest. You may resonate with a similar country type's popular sports, types of business, or even religion.

Religion and Type

You may be able to find the religion that fits your type the best. A few Asians commented that Buddhism is quiet and compassionate—both facets of introversion and feeling. I was raised in the American Christian tradition and lived for three years in Japan. The Eastern Asian religions (including Japan) are Mahayana Buddhism and Confucianism. I have never been to Nepal or India but I have spent several months in Thailand.

My dominant introverted feeling was attracted to Thailand's Theravada Buddhism. I am not a Buddhist but the Theravada Buddhist religion in Thailand has resonated with my inner self more than Christianity or Mahayana Buddhism. Once again, I have two preferences in common with Thailand, one with Japan and none with the USA. Through type you may find the religion that evokes your deepest interest.

I have found ethnicity, language and religion are key factors in determining and separating type groups. In the western world, Catholic countries tend to be FP (introverted feeling) with a small minority of TP (introverted thinking). Protestant countries tend to be SJ (introverted sensing). It is interesting to note both Protestants and SJ (introverted sensing) types are know for their work ethic.

Protestant southern and eastern regions of Africa tend to be ESFJ (extraverted feeling and introverted sensing). Orthodox countries tend to be ENP (extraverted intuition).

In the eastern world, Theravada and Tibetan Buddhist countries tend to be FP (introverted feeling) and Mahayana Buddhist, Confucianist, and Taoist countries tend to be SJ (introverted sensing). Hindu countries (India and Nepal) are NFP (extraverted intuition and introverted feeling).

The majority of Islamic countries tend to be ESP (extraverted sensing) with a small percentage that are ENP (extraverted intuition). African countries that are ESFP (extraverted sensing and introverted feeling) are a mix of Animism, Muslim and Christian religions. Oceania/Pacific Islands are ESFP and are a mix of Animism and ancestor worshiping, and ones that were converted to Christianity (both Protestant and Catholic).

The dominant mental processes of Islamic, Animistic and Orthodox religions tend to be more perceiving types (EP, IJ), whereas Protestants tend to be more judging types (EJ, IP). Catholics, Buddhists and Hindus are split between perceiving and judging. Once again, if out of balance, perceiving types may have poorly defined values and principles and at the extreme no ethics, whereas judging types can be blind to new facts, new ideas and at the extreme one-track, close-minded, rigid and judgmental.

Lastly, is there any possibility that the ethnic conflict with Muslims in Europe is because there is such a wide gap between country types? There are only a few ESP countries in Europe yet the majority of Islamic countries tend to be ESP.

5

Type Bias

When my brother was visiting Amsterdam, a Dutch girl rejected his advances by claiming the US has no culture. She had hit our weak spot as Americans. My brother came back to me and asked what are some examples of great contributions by Americans to high culture. We struggled to find some. Maybe Mark Twain?

Ironically, this was the same question the Foreign Service Officers asked me during the US Foreign Service Officer oral exam. I'm sure they have been confronted with this question more than once themselves. There is no good answer because it is the weak spot of our ESTJ culture they have hit it upon. In our extraverted thinking American culture, we have grown up with an appreciation of business and mechanics instead of the arts, humanities and social sciences. In the extreme, travel writer Paul Theroux (who lives part-time in Hawaii) said the people in Hawaii would probably chew on a book before reading one.

Country type means that people in a culture tend to show a preference for and reward certain behaviors. These cultural expectations are transmitted throughout society (in the family, community, workplace etc) and reinforced by the media and television.

I was brought up in the extraverted thinking culture of the USA. As a result, I had less of a chance to develop my feeling preference and it became a weak spot (an immature, undeveloped func-

tion). On the other hand, a thinking type growing up in American culture has more of a chance of developing tunnel vision because they haven't been forced to use other functions (like their feeling function) as often.

Another example of a weak spot is the Japanese imagination. The Japanese have a preference for being realistic therefore the opposite facet of imagination is a weak spot. Many English teachers ask Japanese students to use their imagination on their assignments but get weak results. Professors bring in someone's picture and tell them to write about the person's work, life, and everything using their imagination. This is a very hard exercise for the Japanese. Using your imagination is not encouraged in Japanese culture because they are they are realistic, sensing types.

When you grow up in a particular culture type, you develop an enhanced awareness and ability with that function. Therefore, growing up in American culture I learned how to be extroverted thinking even though it's my fourth function and not normally developed in my type until around age fifty. Normally, my extroverted thinking would be inferior, immature and undeveloped but it is much stronger from growing up in the US.

The same goes for Hawaii, as an extraverted sensing culture people in general have an ability to use extroverted sensing more than on the mainland US. Extraverted sensing types notice more

in the surrounding environment than other types because their five senses are fully tuned into the present moment. People in Hawaii have a heightened sense of awareness of the people around them. Their extroverted sensing can see subtle reactions and actions of others. They pay attention to details and are practiced at reading a person's face.

Myers

"Western civilization has inclined men toward thinking, women toward feeling, and both sexes toward extraversion and the judging attitude. The pressure of outer circumstance itself would seem to be toward sensing. Thus anyone who came into the world as a clean slate would be likely to be marked ESTJ or ESFJ fairly promptly by the collective slate pencil, which may explain why there are so many ESTJs and ESFJs in the general population.

Against that view, type theory would argue that readiness to accept and enforce conformity is an essential part of the inner disposition of ESTJs and ESFJs. Thus, the prevalence of these types could be a cause, not a result, of some of the more materialistic social pressures of our times." (Myers, *Gifts Differing*)

In addition to social pressure, Myers believed a lack of faith, acceptance, opportunity and incentive are obstacles to people developing their own type. Culture is about social pressure and environmental expectations. Culture tells us which personality type is accepted, given opportunities and incentives. If the socially accepted personality type isn't ours, we may lack faith in our natural inner preferences.

Culture Type Bias

I once heard someone say that type tells you what to do and culture tells you how to do it. I have to disagree. If you are the same type as the culture type then there are plenty of avenues to express your type. If you are the opposite type, there is a void. No explanations just implications that you should act more like the culture type.

For example, in America as an introvert you are marginalized if not outright discriminated against. When I presented my book idea to Americans their first reaction was that I should go out and do public presentations on my topic or sell my services as a trainer to corporations going global. They didn't realize it but this was an unconscious and complete discount of the fact that I am an introvert. Part of this ignorance is a lack of education in the US on what introversion is. Introverts are a minority (about 25%-33% of the US

population) and aren't socially accepted—sometimes to the point of discrimination.

Some introverts spend their whole career in an extraverted job. I know four university professors that are very introverted like me. They teach engineering, foreign language, business and psychology. When I was considering getting my PhD, I told one of them that I don't like speaking in front of others. He told me he didn't either (he is an excellent professor by the way) but he said you draw up an outline from your textbook of what you will say to each class and just follow that.

The psychology professor (INFP) said that's why introvert professors would like to have the chairs in rows and nailed to the floor.

There aren't people moving chairs around and interacting with each other, just the professor at the front of the room lecturing the whole hour. Another professor (INTJ) said 'you just do it', you develop an ability to be the extravert that the position demands.

As an introvert in junior high school I wasn't able to 'just do it' and flunked speech class. After college I unwittingly got into sales and was miserable. If I had grown up in an introverted culture I might have been more in tune with my type but American culture taught me it's good to be gregarious and outgoing, the guy that attracts other people to him and is loved to be around.

Living in Japan I found it acceptable to be an introvert. Although a lot of my Japanese students (especially the adults) were expecting me to be the loud, funny, stereotypical American. Even my wife told me I am more like a Japanese in this respect than an American. She also said Japanese feel let down when an American doesn't act extraverted.

6

Equal Reward For Gifts Differing

The majority of the western world is extroverted thinking type cultures. Capitalism is a product of extroverted thinking type cultures. Thinking cultures (ESTJ, ISTJ) are home to the majority of the biggest global companies. According to Fortune magazine, out of the top 500 global corporations, 170 are from the USA.

Thinking types can be competitive, impersonal, tough-minded and tend to see progress and results as more important than people considerations. Feeling types can be tender, gentle, and see the world on a personal level. Feeling types empathize with the negative effect of globalization on individuals and communities.

"At the heart of globalisation is a new kind of intolerance in the west towards other cultures, traditions and values, less brutal than in the era of colonialism, but more comprehensive and totalitarian. The idea that each culture is possessed of its own specific wisdom and characteristics, its own novelty and uniqueness, born of its own individual struggle over thousands of years to cope with nature and circumstance, has been drowned out by the hue and cry that the world is now one, that the western model—neoliberal markets, democracy and the rest—is the template for all."—Martin Jacques, April 17, 2006, *The Guardian*.

Each personality type has a dark side or shadow which is an undeveloped, immature side of the personality type. It is the weaker or inferior functions but it can also be a result of relying too heavily on the favorite function. Projecting our own weaknesses (and any parts of our type that we repress) on others is one form of the being possessed by the dark side. Each of the eight mental processes have different dark sides, one may become judging, whereas another might become blaming, and another controlling, etc.

In American culture and the capitalist/globalist system, there also resides the dark side or weakness of the extroverted thinking type. The dark side of the extroverted thinking country type can be a stifling of voices contrary to its self-determined intellectual truth (economic and political), and at worst exploiting and discriminating against non-extroverted thinking type countries.

There is nothing wrong with commerce and trade until it is used to exploit people, destroy culture, and rob natural resources, property and land from other people. Another example is in the US, where inequality of wealth is huge and still growing (see inequality. org). This gap between the rich and the poor is part of the dark side of the extroverted thinking culture—tunneling so deeply into thinking that the feeling function is repressed.

Misconceptions and Myths

Capitalism and globalism have been lumped together with democracy because they have some similar looking goals like freedom and freedom of the market place—but this is a misconception. Capitalism is the dark rider on the white horse of democracy. Capitalist organizations and systems do not serve the needs of the people. By the nature of the beast they can only be loyal to profits, competition, and leveraging the law and lawmakers.

One person from Mongolia commented that Mongolians were becoming more early-starting (J), and that they were "sharply growing up now due to whole economy changes." Several Europeans mentioned their culture changing as a result of the recent globalization.

There is a myth that other countries just need to grow up and become economically productive. Focus on productivity is an extroverted thinking trait. This myth discounts what is valued by other country types. For example, feeling type countries place the welfare of people before economic and productivity goals.

Feeling is the weak spot of thinking type western cultures. Individuals usually don't develop a weaker function unless they are in circumstances that force them to. What circumstances will bring this about in the US and western cultures? Wars? The increasing gap between the rich and the poor?

Feeling type individuals and feeling type countries have the sensitivity, human concern, and humanitarianism necessary to right the injustice done by totalitarian rule of the capitalists and globalists. Feeling type countries make up more than three quarters of the world. They must find their voice despite being disempowered by the prevailing thinking type economic and political systems or face the repeating scenario of colonization and globalization that steals power and land from under people, like the feeling type Hawaiians who became a small, powerless, landless minority on their own islands and to this day are still are not recognized by the American government.

The dark side of the extroverted thinking type countries can be intolerant and totalitarian, but one Tibetan student saw a silver lining on the storm cloud of globalization. International students find an interest in their ethnic culture when coming to an international community like East-West Center. She felt sometimes globalization doesn't erode culture but can sparks renewed interest in it. By encountering a new culture you become even more aware of your own cultural upbringing.

Ethnic minorities growing up in a large city in China don't strongly identity with their ethnic culture and heritage. These minorities go to other countries (to study, etc.) and encounter other cultures. They find a renewed interest in their own ethnic culture—even though they didn't know it growing up in a large city.

A New Paradigm - Equal Opportunity and Equal Reward for Gifts Differing

Companies try to improve performance by putting 'the square pegs (people) in the square holes'. But this is only the beginning; the future for the 'gifts differing' philosophy is equal reward for different gifts. Imagine the power of not only giving people the opportunity to use their gifts but also rewarding them equally for their gifts. Empower people with the dignity to use their unique gifts and be rewarded.

All people are created equal including their unique gifts and should all be compensated equally. No gift is 'more equal' or important than another. This is the antithesis of capitalism where no man is equal and every man has equal opportunity to have his gift ignored or exploited—by not being given an opportunity to use his/ her gift or by giving the rewards of his gift to someone else.

Globalism brings people from different countries together but we should be concerned if capitalism is the mechanism by which the world is brought together. Under capitalism not all people are given a chance to use their gifts and not all gifts are rewarded. Capitalism, even at its best, is the antithesis to the philosophy of equal opportunity and equal reward for gifts differing.

C.G. Jung believed the universal truths gleaned by the introvert processes (from the collective unconscious) will not be realized until they become commonly accepted knowledge. For those that are religious, Jung believed the collective unconscious is where god resides. So universal truths might be equated with messages from god. Universal truths apply to everyone no matter what religion. Therefore, capitalism and its international equivalent globalism will crumble as the universal truth of equal opportunity and equal reward for gifts differing is accepted into mainstream knowledge as common sense.

7

ENFJ—Extraverted Feeling plus Introverted Intuition

Descriptions of culture and national character correspond easily with personality type preferences, interests, traits and behavior, but the real magic of the four-letter code is indicating the favored mental process.

The next two chapters are about the extraverted feeling mental process. ENFJs and ESFJs prefer to use extraverted feeling the majority of the time. Their second choice, in the case of the ENFJ would be introverted intuition, and for the ESFJ introverted sensing. It is good to keep the mental processes in mind when reading the country profiles.

Thinking vs Feeling countries

According to type expert Ray Moody, feeling types wear clothing with horizontal lines or horizontal patterns and thinking types wear clothing with vertical lines or verticle patterns. In Japan clothing with horizontal lines is quite popular and Japan is a feeling type culture. My wife noticed that in the US more people like to wear vertical lined clothing compared to Japan. This isn't surprising because the US is a thinking type country. My extraverted feeling wife loves horizontal lined clothing but felt kind of weird wearing it in the US.

ENFJs use extraverted feeling and have a secondary preference for introverted intuition. We all use extraverted feeling when we

take care others and strive for harmony in relationships. However, the ENFJ uses it more and is likely to be better at it than other types. Extraverted feeling is what ENFJs use in the outer world and for interactions with others. ENFJs second preference is for introverted intuition. Introverted intuitive types have occasional flashes of insight or visions into what the future will hold. ENFJs use introverted intuition in their inner, private world so it's difficult to observe in their actions or words.

NORTH AMERICA

Quebec, Canada is ENFJ:

Clear				Slight				Clear
I				▓	▓	▓		E
N			▓					S
F	▓	▓	▓					T
P				▓				J

French Canadian culture also is reflective (I), experiential (S), casual (P) and open-ended (P). (The end of Chapter 2 has a decription of each facet.)

Based on discussions with several Quebeckers, they responded with the following comments: "I think it is important to keep in mind the fact Canada was founded by two different colonies and two distinct cultures. As a native French speaker, I can see the differences. Globally, English speaking Canada is much more like USA. Our nation, Quebec, is much more 'libertine' than the average English speaking Canada. We are more open to foreigners (Quebec has its own immigration system, especially open to Latin Americans who do not meet qualifications for Canadian standards)."

French Canadians first and foremost are extraverted feeling types and as such are "more tender, accepting and accommodating. For example, think of gays and lesbians' rights and the choice of abortion. We believe in fairness and equality, we are respectful towards differences (Montreal being in the top 5 gay destinations, having their own 'Olympic games' set in Montreal).For instance, it has been considered that Ontario could have their own Sharia (Islamic) courts, as being an accepting nation. In many other countries, as Australia, this possibility would not even be considered. Quebeckers can trust people too easily. They could be more cautious."

"Because of their status as a minority, Quebeckers have no choice but to be accommodating. A good example is that they have coined the term 'reasonable accommodation' in the area of human rights." As feeling types, "Quebeckers are very loyal to language, culture and friends."

"If you compare our minority, Quebec, we remained quieter than the majority of other independence-seeking nations (Vasco, Montenegro, etc.) and tried to achieve it in peace (except for the FLQ in 1970)." This also is an example of an extraverted feeling type considering others and maintaining harmony. Lastly, as feeling types, "We care strongly about environment and act in this way (Quebec is ratifying Kyoto's Protocol while Canada dropped it; we recycle and compost, avoid using disposable items—cups, forks, etc.)"

French Canadians are intuitive types. "Quebeckers generally are good orators and capable of abstract ideas and intellectual debates.

In the Francophonie, Quebec writers publish more books and novels than any other group. Quebeckers have always had to be inventive and imaginative, especially because they are a minority in Canada, they have no choice but to be novel."

They have a slight preference for intuition, therefore also use sensing by relying on direct experience instead of theories. "While they are intellectually inclined, Quebeckers, like Americans, like to test their ideas and will insist on experience or theory and practice as being inseparable. In education, programs with work and studies combined are more and more popular. Theories are seen as ideologies and opinions. Experience on the field is most important. Action is important. Education, for example, is more and more based on employment and less on acquiring general knowledge or being able to think and judge a situation. If knowledge is not useful for the potential job-acquiring it is a waste of time."

Also, as intuitive types, they reject convention, "You could say the French nation in Canada is nothing traditional, especially if you compare it to the rest of North America. Tradition is seen as old and not useful. People must innovate all the time in enterprise for example. Science is seen as a more valuable source of information than tradition. In Quebec, most of the women in the 1970s were told to give their babies powder milk, breast milk was not as good for the infant. Still in 2006 only 50% in Quebec (outside Quebec 85%) of women breastfeed their babies. Scientific innovation is central and for most people the key to new challenges like environmental problems (science will save us all). Quebeckers like their traditions but they are also very much interested in new things. They can set trends in clothes, food, readings."

English Canadians said, "The French Canadians will tell you anything on their mind." French Canadians are extraverts. "Quebeckers are very easy to get to know and good conversationalists. Most people from popular classes and middle class will talk about their private life in public. People will even go on television to talk about private manners. For Francophones they will use the 'tu' (the less formal French translation of 'you', used for people you are familiar with) easily even if they do not know the person. For

Anglophone they will tend to use your first name rapidly. French Canadians will laugh loudly in public and demonstrate their emotion without being ashamed. They usually like to be in groups and chat for hours in cafés or even in their kitchens."

"Quebeckers are usually gregarious people. They like to meet others. Quebeckers do not hesitate to talk to people in the streets. Most people are open to visitors. Neighbors will talk to each other and will introduce themselves when you're new. People with many friends seem like a good person. Someone introverted who enjoys being alone is seen as anti-social or weird sometimes."

French Canadians have a slight preference for judging, therefore also enjoy being causal and open-ended. "Anglophones and Francophones in Canada are different on that point. Francophones have more of the Latin background (relaxed, easygoing and extraverted). Like most people in North America, Quebeckers are relaxed and easy going. They like to eat well and chat in cafés. Quebeckers are generally easy with life. They accept going with the flow. Quebeckers are spontaneous. They react positively to the unexpected especially in regard to meals. We usually say when guests arrive uninvited that if there is enough for four, there will be enough for five."

Greenland is ENFJ:

	Clear				Slight			Clear	
I					▓	▓			E
N		▓	▓						S
F	▓	▓	▓						T
P					▓				J

Greenlandic culture also is intimate (I), traditional (S), casual (P), and open-ended (P). The last three are the same as Quebec.

According to one Greenlander, "Greenland and the Faroe Islands are part of the Kingdom of Denmark since 1700s. Culturally & linguistically speaking, the Danes and Greenlanders are very different." Most Greenlanders have both Eskimo and Scandinavian ancestry, and speak Greenlandic as their first language (but also speak English and Danish). Greenland has a population of 56,000 and the majority of the population is Evangelical Lutheran.

I received only two responses from Greenland and they differed on judging and perceiving. The city of Qaanaaq in the north is perceiving (ENFP) and Sisimiut in the south is judging (ENFJ). Southern Greenland and Quebec (French Canada) are geographically close and the same type—ENFJ. Northern Greenland is the same as Denmark—ENFP. The Eskimos of the Arctic Circle (Alaska, Canada, and Russia) are culturally similar, so ENFP might be the type for all the Eskimos in the Artic circle.

One foreigner living in Qaanaaq replied, "It is the northernmost town in Greenland, which is a small community of 650 (900 including the surrounding settlements). The ways of living here are based largely on a hunting culture." She commented about the people being resourceful and embracing the new and modern (intuitive) yet also being traditional. "People are extremely intelligent and resourceful. I think that one of the reasons is that they are used to making by themselves what they need. One example: some tourists were marveling that hunters on a hunting trip were repairing a harpoon head using an old teaspoon (flattening the material and sharpening it). 'Why don't they go back to town to buy a new one?' A tourist asked. But all harpoon heads are handmade by the hunter. He used a spoon because he had no other material in the field, but this is just a small everyday chore for a local hunter."

"People love new and modern things. Almost all the teenagers here have mobile phones, families that live in settlements without TV connection have DVDs, etc. On the other hand, I marvel at their ability to choose between technology and tradition. For example, no snowmobiles are used here for hunting. Hunting in the cold season is done 100% by dogsled. Any hunter will tell you that only a dogteam can catch the scent of a polar bear or take you home safely in a blizzard. Narwhal whales are hunted by kayak and harpoon, because the sound of motor boats scare narwhal away, and if you shoot at them with rifles, you will injure or lose many animals, but if you harpoon them, none are ever lost because we use a sealskin float attached to the harpoon head. Only the Eskimos in northern

Greenland still live mainly by hunting seals and continue to follow many of their traditional ways."

This person also commented on the nature of the weather as an example of the intangible aspect (intuitive) of the culture. "I feel that this may be something that originates from the hunting culture of the High Arctic. One of the first things anyone learns (whether you are a tourist, outsider come to live here, or small child born to a local family) is that the weather is the ultimate boss. Basics of life follow the weather conditions and movement of animals. Nobody here will make an appointment for tomorrow, because it is not right to make a promise to go hunting together when you can never be sure what the weather will be like tomorrow. (This is not true in people engaged in office work, but lingers very strongly in private life.)"

Greenlanders are feeling types. "The general feeling between people is basically warm. We don't see the dis-attachment that you can see in many modern metropolitans. Acceptance and respect towards differences in another person or culture is a basic attitude in most people. People are very tolerant and praising, especially towards children."

"Basically, people are quite shy. However, the people in Avanersuaq (Thule district) are extremely generous, open and sociable when they feel that the other party is of their own kind, or understands or shares their values. In the case of Greenlanders, this usually happens when the other party is family members, close friends, or visitors from a different place (the definition of family members here is much broader than the average western sense. Distant family members are welcomed very warmly, and that can be one third of the population if it is a small settlement). In the case of outsiders (foreign people), this happens towards people who show a respect towards the native culture and have the will to blend in."

They report themselves as extraverts. "Public meetings, broad circles, or just a big gathering that happened naturally, are quite often. Such gatherings are part of the culture and social life, and have been like this for probably centuries. The sense of humor of these people is just wonderful!"

Greenlanders are split between judging and perceiving. They have a preference for being casual and open-ended. "If the weather turns bad, you have to go home even if you don't have any prey, for the sake of safety. People take in the situation as is comes and changes—even now for different matters (than hunting)."

EUROPE

French-speaking Belgium is ENFJ:

Clear				Slight			Clear
I				▓	▓	▓	E
N			▓				S
F			▓				T
P				▓			J

French-speaking Belgian culture also is concrete (S), traditional (S), reasonable (T), and critical (T).

Dutch-speaking Belgium is ISFP:

Clear				Slight			Clear
I			▓				E
N				▓			S
F				▓			T
P		▓					J

Dutch-speaking Belgian culture also is active (E), abstract (N), imaginative (N), empathic (F), and scheduled (J).

"Remember there is one country but two subcultures Flemish (Dutch-speaking, North) and Walloon (French-speaking, South)" also the eastern border is German speaking. About 60 percent of the country is Dutch-speaking, 39 percent French-speaking, and 1 percent German-speaking. Brussels, with 8% of the country's population, is officially bilingual (French-Dutch).

"We Belgians are confused and probably also confusing." The responses I received were confusing but I speculate French-speaking Belgium is ExFJ and Flemish (Dutch-speaking) is ISxP (with the 'x' meaning it was split).

"The Dutch-speaking population is more (and appreciates more) likely to be reasonable, trustful, to apply principles and cause-and-effect analyses, in contrast to the French-speaking population that is more compassionate, tactful, sympathetic, and loyal" (thinking vs feeling).

"The Dutch-speaking population is more (and appreciates more) likely to be unconventional, original, new and unusual" (the same as the Dutch in the Netherlands), "in contrast to the French-speaking population that is more traditional and conventional" (the same as the French in France).

One Dutch speaker stated the French-speaking Belgians and Dutch-speaking Belgians are generally opposite on introversion and extraversion but more or less the same for the rest of the preferences. "This has everything to do with the late 16th century divide between the protestant North (Holland) and the Counter-Reformist South; Flemings and Walloons are subcultures of a largely Catholic culture and the differences between them are less significant than between Belgians and Dutch."

"I am a Dutch-speaking Belgian so this maybe had some influence but I do not think that it is major. For me, Belgians are Belgians and not Dutch- or French-speaking. Belgians have their own character. Which does not mean that there aren't many differences for we represent two folk types, Romanic and Germanic. Both the Dutch-speaking and French-speaking are social persons and bon-vivants." Bon-vivant is a sensing trait.

One Dutch-speaker made a comment that sounded introverted and perceiving: "Social, relaxed, maybe a bit reserved in the beginning and modest. That's how I see us, Belgians. Sometimes also a little confused, gullible. But most of all a bon-vivant. Something typical for Belgium is the solution 'à la belge' (said both in Flanders and Wallonia, and is translated 'with the Belgian'). A solution that all know isn't a good one, but it's a solution and that's how it will be for now. And all have the intention that it will only be a temporary solution but all know that this probably will be a long-term solution anyway. An okay idea but we are 'too lazy' to think it over until it's a good one."

Another Dutch-speaker made an introverted and sensing type comment: "Easy going, rather modest and simple. Focus on own house & family. Frequent contact and events with friends and within family are very important. The Belgian is rather an individual, sometimes alternative traveler (no comparison with Germans,

British, Dutch). Rather calm and peaceful mind. Can appreciate simple things, which are making part of a *joie de vivre* (like to live). Foible for good food and drinks: champagne (2nd biggest consumption/capita in world), wines (world's best wine cellars outside France to be found are in Belgium), beer (speaks for itself). Belgium has been changing from a extreme conservative, administrative and hierarchical society into a very liberal and tolerant one."

AFRICA

Ghana is ENFJ:

Clear				Slight			Clear
I				▓	▓	▓	E
N			▓				S
F	▓	▓	▓				T
P				▓			J

Ghanaian culture also is concrete (N), traditional (S), pressure-prompted (P), and spontaneous (P).

Only one person reported on Ghana, and other African countries are ESFP and ESFJ so I am still undecided on Ghana's type.

8

ESFJ—Extraverted Feeling plus Introverted Sensing

ESFJs use extraverted feeling and have a secondary preference for introverted sensing. We all use extraverted feeling when we take care of others and strive for harmony in relationships. However, the ESFJ uses it more and is likely to be better at it than other types. Extraverted feeling is what ESFJs use in the outer world and with interactions with others. ESFJs second preference is for introverted sensing. Introverted sensors relate the here-and-now with their past experiences. ESFJs use introverted sensing in their inner, private world so it's difficult to observe in their actions or words.

Feeling is the dominant mental process of the ESFJs and it is extraverted. The extraverted feeling type takes its value system from the community and people that surround them almost to a point that they sometimes don't really know what they personally value. They rely on the outside world to tell them that. In the extreme they can even appear to blow with the wind, ever changing with their moods and interpretations of what society expects. They aren't to be blamed because their desire for harmony and belonging are really their true inner values. They value others above themselves and dedicate themselves to the welfare of the people around them.

My wife, an ESFJ, when growing up, desired sensing things (e.g. new clothes, etc,) but as an extravert feeling type she knew that her family didn't have a lot of money so she held back. Her sister is an

ISFJ and as an introverted sensor had less of a problem requesting from her parents all sorts of things like new clothes. Her extraverted feeling didn't stop her dominant sensing from speaking up. My wife always felt she wanted to be like her sister in this manner but her feeling process always kept her introverted sensing pushed down below the surface, or repressed. Now that she is an adult (and living away from her family) she feels more confidence voicing her sensing desires. She has developed her introverted sensing as she has grown older. She found she could use it with more maturity and therefore had more confidence expressing it. As we grow older we develop our second preference and eventually later in life our third and fourth.

Introverted Sensing

An introverted sensing type takes time to absorb and understand the sensory experiences they are recording. In terms of which sense is easiest to record to memory, my ESFJ wife said her visual is the strongest, then hearing, and then speaking. She also needs some down time to file what she has recorded. Introverted mental processes work best when they have some private time. Introverted sensing types see, hear, feel, etc. something and it triggers mental associations with past events.

ESFJs use introverted sensing in service to their extraverted feeling (and not the other way around). My ESFJ wife, as an extraverted feeling type, only mentions her good mental associations (from her introverted sensing). She tells them to amuse and make people laugh. She will even tell her own failures if they are amusing. She will also amuse people with her silly associations of 'this is similar to that' or other comparisons. She wants to make them laugh. She tells humorous associations to others, such as when she got some photos back from developing and thought she was looking at her father's face but it was hers. She also looks for people's good points and other good things to praise—like if they got a haircut or did something nice. She does this because she knows how she likes this too. Her self-esteem is low and it raises her self-esteem and others self-esteem.

NORTH AMERICA

Canada (English-speaking) is ESFJ:

Clear				Slight			Clear
I				░	░		E
N				░	░		S
F		░	░				T
P				░			J

Canadian (English) culture also is conceptual (N), imaginative (N), reasonable (T), and casual (P). (The end of Chapter 2 has a decription of each facet.)

"It is very hard to classify Canadians in general. Perhaps that is because of the diversity found in Canada. Compared to most other countries, we are really not homogenous ethnically or religiously. If I had to pick one Canadian trait, I think it is a strong belief in freedom of expression. We really do not encourage people to adopt common beliefs or values but to think for themselves. In my opinion, this results in the wide range of views & values that can be found in Canada and it is this diversity that makes Canada very unique."

"If you are looking for common traits which are uniquely Canadian...possibly it would be the way we define ourselves as being different from Americans. (We did not have much choice about who our neighbours are.) A sure way to offend a Canadian is to ask them what part of America they are from. Sure Canadian culture and media is heavily influenced by our southern neighbours, so I guess we have to concentrate on the differences to retain our uniqueness. For example, there was an advertisement for a beer called 'Canadian' a few years back. It became a nationwide hit. View at the following link: http://www.coolcanuckaward.ca/joe_canadian.htm"

Since Canadian culture is ESFJ and American culture is ESTJ, the biggest culture clash could be between a Canadian preference for feeling and an American preference for thinking. I met three Canadians that hailed from the large cities of Toronto and Vancouver. One of the first things they said is that Canadians aren't as materialistic as Americans. I am apt to classify that as a thinking vs feeling difference but I haven't seen any research on that.

Canadians are extraverts. Some Canadians felt Jim Carey was a classic example of the expressive Canadian. "Many people I know are very outgoing, initiate contact with strangers, like the spotlight, etc. These people are naturally that way and I don't think it reflects their culture or ethnic background. However, there are ethnic factors to consider and as someone who has traveled all over the world, I can attest to the fact that there are definite cultural differences. Germans and Brits, for example, tend to be more reserved while the Irish and Latin Americans are generally very warm and friendly."

Canadians are sensing types. "Two examples of how Canadians are Traditional—conventional, customary, tried-and-true rather than Original—unconventional, different, new and unusual:

1. Several provinces continue to use provincial government operated liquor monopolies run under the title Liquor Control Board when their main function is to increase liquor sales. Despite the fact that Canadians have embraced the metric system and same sex marriage, most Canadians find the obsolete liquor monopolies to be the normal way of doing business and do not press for change.

2. 47% of Canadians would vote to retain the monarchy although 100% of Canadians support the maple leaf flag."

Canadians are sensing types but they also have a sense of imagination (intuition). One Canadian commented, "Who is more resourceful than a Canadian?"

First and foremost Canadians are extraverted feeling types. Canadian's cultural awareness and sensitivity to racism are examples of their feeling preference for being accepting and accommodating. A group of Canadians from Toronto and Vancouver said Canadians are more culturally aware. There is a great mix of people in Canada and many people trace their roots. They know their family's origin, e.g. from Norway, Russia etc.

However, "Many 'born and raised' Canadians find questions about their ethnicity offensive, especially on forms and surveys. That is something that is not quite grasped outside Canada. It is not because we are overly patriotic like the American people. It is because of our, generally speaking, aversion to anything racist. Asking about a person's ethnicity sets the stage, either consciously or unconsciously, for racist divisions. Even subdividing data by ethnicity for statistical purposes is frowned upon."

"While living and working in Bermuda, I and several other Canadians were asked to fill out a nationwide workplace survey form. One of the questions regarded ethnicity. All of the Canadians abstained answering the question in some way or another, because in Canada no one is allowed to ask questions like that on any official survey, job interview, or any other official document/form. Race, religion, or any other personal 'preference' should not be an issue for anything official."

"If you want to ask a Canadian about their family history and background, that is fine and encouraged. My roots derive from the Mennonite migration from the Ukraine after religious persecution by the Russian White Army. The Mennonites moved to Canada because they were promised religious freedom and land. That was a few generations before my time though."

"Canada is a country made up mostly of immigrants. It is similar to New Zealand in that way but with a longer history and in many ways, more diverse. All Canadians are encouraged to retain the cultural identity and traditions that they or their ancestors brought with them from their homeland. They are also encouraged to learn about the history of other Canadians and what brought them to Canada."

There is a "Canadian attitude where the 'local ways' are to respect the individual's culture and everyone is not expected to act the same way. Sure, Canadians sometimes joke about immigrants, but we do not expect them to change who they are or how they act. The winter climate often dictates how they dress, so that is not much of an issue either. This does not mean racists and bigots do not exist in Canada. Unfortunately they do, but their views are not widely shared, especially in the media. Probably the most significant division in Canadian society is between the English and the French."

"There is still discrimination and some acrimony (particularly between the English and the French), but it is far less prevalent than in other places I have been. It is really in the past 20 years that real progress has been made. I think it is partly because my generation was raised during a time when Canada's Charter of Human Rights and anti-discrimination laws began to be really enforced. This was coupled with education. Racism is a learned behaviour. I think my generation was the first to be taught that it is totally unacceptable. The media also played a big role. Canadian media is very conscientious about the issue. Eventually the message filters through. It doesn't happen overnight though, and I certainly did not realise the full extent of the progress made until I started traveling and living in other countries."

"My wife and I are very careful about how we describe people, because it is in the obvious ways to differentiate people that discrimination begins. If you always choose to describe people according to their skin colour or ethnicity, not in a malicious way but just because it is an easy way to describe that person, that automatically validates the differentiation, which sets the stage for further problems. It is a very subtle thing, but very important when shaping developing minds. In some ways it is like the way Orwell in the book 1984, suggested that by removing words from a language you could change the way people think. Not all that far fetched really."

Canadians are also empathic (feeling) and seek to understand others. "There also is the side of the Canadian culture where people are encouraged to consider other people's opinions and respect them. It is good to be confident in your own opinions but the 'My way is right' is to some degree frowned upon. Unfortunately religion is the big stumbling block here."

Canadians have a slight preference for judging, so sometimes they are perceiving. One Canadian gave the example of a hockey pick-up game as an example of making flexible plans.

There is a large Chinese immigrant population in Canada (especially Vancouver). One Chinese-Canadian who grew up in London, Ontario, but was born in Beijing, China, reported the Chinese subculture in Canada as ESFJ—the same type as Canadian culture. I hazard to guess that this is the result of the Canadian culture being so accepting or proof that some immigrants adopt their host country's culture type.

Chinese-Canadians prefer to be extravert. "Our culture promotes success and rising to the top no matter what your background—this trait of being 'Active' is considered essential for achieving this goal." But they have also retained many of the classic Chinese traits. They value being calm and quiet: "Chinese parents want their children to be good citizens that don't get themselves into trouble."

Chinese-Canadians are sensing like the general Canadian culture. "Chinese parents don't have as much patience for abstract ideas—they want the facts. Many immigrants came from poor backgrounds, so they are very realistic in their approach about life—they

can't afford to spend time 'day-dreaming'. Chinese immigrants generally only follow practices that they know have worked instead of taking 'unnecessary' risks. Some immigrants know what it's like to be dirt-poor so they are all about being realistic and doing things for a purpose—they're not as accepting as established Canadians with money about experimenting." For Chinese-Canadians tradition (sensing) is tied to harmony (feeling). "Chinese immigrants can be very rooted in tradition—thus they want their children to just accept what they, 'the elders', say and not argue."

The Chinese also have a preference for intuition (intellectual) when it relates to education. "Many immigrants, Chinese immigrants in particular, highly value education as a means of advancing forward in life. The emphasis is on being intellectual and succeeding in school instead of more physical endeavors."

CENTRAL AMERICA

Costa Rica is ESFJ:

Clear				Slight			Clear	
I				■				E
N				■				S
F		■	■					T
P				■				J

Costa Rican culture also is contained (I), intimate (I), conceptual (N), theoretical (N), reasonable (T), open-ended (P), and pressure-prompted (P).

"In general we get along pretty well with almost everybody. Probably Americans, Canadians, and Western Europeans are the people Costa Ricans identify easily with. We have some issues with some Central American countries due to the vast amount of immigration we have received over the years, so, it can be said that the relationship with Nicaraguans especially has not always been the best. However, in general, it is very cordial. As far as the rest of Latin America, it is basically the same: a good but some times distant relationship." Costa Rica is the only ESFJ country in Central America. Their extroverted feeling tendency to caretake and be concerned with the welfare of others may be getting taken advantage of.

EUROPE

Ukraine is ESFJ:

Clear				Slight			Clear	
I				■	■	■		E
N				■				S
F			■					T
P				■				J

Ukrainian culture also is abstract (N), reasonable (T), tough (T), open-ended (P), and pressure-prompted.

AFRICA

Burkina Faso is ESFJ:

Clear				Slight				Clear
I				▓	▓	▓		E
N				▓	▓	▓		S
F			▓					T
P				▓	▓			J

Burkinabe culture also is logical (T), reasonable (T), and casual (P).

French is the official language of Burkina Faso.The ethnic groups are more than Mossi (40%), also Gurunsi, Senufo, Lobi, Bobo, Mande, and Fulani. Approximately 50% of the population is Muslim; Christians (Roman Catholic) account for about 30%, and followers of traditional African religions (typically animism of various forms) make up about 20%. Many Christians and Muslims incorporate elements of animism into their religious practices. The Christian countries in Africa tended to be ESFJ, therefore this may represent Burkinabe Christians.

Mozambique is ESFJ:

Clear				Slight				Clear
I				▓	▓	▓		E
N				▓	▓			S
F			▓					T
P				▓				J

Mozambican culture also is imaginative (N), logical (T), casual (P) and open-ended (P).

Namibia is ESFJ:

Clear				Slight			Clear	
I				■	■			E
N				■	■	■		S
F		■	■					T
P				■				J

Namibian culture also is logical (T), casual (P) and open-ended (P).

Nigeria is ESFJ:

Clear				Slight			Clear	
I				■	■			E
N				■	■	■		S
F	■	■	■					T
P				■				J

Nigerian culture also is conceptual (N), tough (T), casual (P), and open-ended (P).

Northern Nigeria is ENTP:

Clear				Slight			Clear	
I				■	■	■		E
N			■					S
F								T
P	■	■	■					J

Northern Nigerian culture also is experiential (S), traditional (S), and accepting (F).

I interviewed three Nigerians, two reported ESFJ and one ENTP. I speculate these are a split between Protestant (ESFJ) and Muslim (ENTP). Islam dominates in the north and Protestantism predominates in Yoruba areas (southwestern Nigeria). The Yoruba constitute approximately 30 percent of Nigeria's total population.

"Nigeria is the largest black nation in the world." This isn't surprising because they are the ninth most populous nation in the world at 131 million (just above Japan). Nigeria is by far the biggest African nation with 1 in 5 Africans being Nigerian. I talked with a demographer that works for the Nigerian government. He said, "West African countries were French and English colonies. West African people act very much alike and have a similar color. There are a couple hundred tribes in Nigeria with three main ones influencing the culture."

I interviewed a Nigerian man and woman who were nursing students at Hawaii Pacific University (HPU). "Nigeria is considered the Giant of Africa and is the most civilized. There is a mix of 50/50 Muslim and Christian. All the African countries behave the same but just have different food, traditions, clothes etc." One culture researcher (McCrae) said the Africans (and Asians) have less of a deviation from the average. Basically, African people from different African countries tend to act similar to each other. The Nigerians also felt "with Middle Easterners and Indians we don't have to translate or bridge a communication gap like we have to do with Americans and other Westerners."

Nigerians lead with extraverted feeling types and prefer to be personable. "Nigerians have limited personal space and can stand very close to a person, they love touching, and hugging others. They look to friends before professionals on things like career advice." One Nigerian lady was looking for a job and consulting her friend. "I would rather talk to someone I know than go to the college career center where they don't know me and will probably just run down a checklist with me. I want to talk to my friends because they will understand me better, I feel safe with them. The same for a counseling, nobody will see a psychologist, they will talk to a friend instead. However, it is different from a medical doctor. Nigerians will readily go to a hospital because they start to feel better with the doctor touching them."

A Nigerian man from Lagos said, "The capital of Nigeria, is like Mexico, congested and difficult to live in so you learn to be tough." Nigerians prefer the tough facet of thinking because society grooms them that way. "We are raised to have self-discipline and no unnecessary complaining. We have to be ready to face whatever comes.

We can't afford to break down. It is difficult to live in Nigeria with infrastructure problems and political problems making everyday life a challenge." The Nigerian students both recommended a book that explains the tough facet of the culture: *Things Fall Apart* by Chinua Achebe (one of Nigeria's popular authors). They used this book in their social anthropology class. This class was a requirement because nurses must be sensitive to cultural issues. They learned cross-cultural awareness like Micronesians could only be bathed by one of the family and not a nurse. Also, men should not visibly see Middle Eastern women.

Nigeria is like Asia (and SJ types) in the sense of respect. "You don't call your elders and parents by their names. Children are allowed to be seen but not heard—however this is changing. Other forms of respect are never using your left hand to give something to someone or do anything else. There also is a sense of formality in making an acquaintance. You present yourself formally (How do you do, my name is...) and not just start talking to someone like they do here in the USA. However, after living here I have gotten used to the American style of talking to anyone."

Uganda is ESFJ:

Clear				Slight				Clear
I					▓			E
N					▓			S
F	▓	▓	▓	▓				T
P					▓	▓		J

Ugandan culture also is intimate (I) and spontaneous (P).

A lady from the University in Kampala said ESFJ represents the central and south. She said, "The north is more like Nigerians—aggressive and not soft. Someone from Nigeria—you can't step on him, whereas someone from Uganda if you step on him (figuratively) he will keep quiet for the sake of peace. The north is resolved, warrior-like, and they feel suppressed by the south. There has be twenty years of fighting between the north and the south."

Northern Uganda is ESFP:

Clear				Slight			Clear
I				▓	▓		E
N				▓	▓		S
F		▓					T
P		▓					J

Northern Ugandan culture also is intimate (I), imaginative (N), reasonable (T), critical (T), systematic (J), and early starting (J).

A man from Gulu Town in the north commented, "The character of our people in general can be summed up as: warm, social, open and hardworking."

Zimbabwe is ESFJ:

Clear				Slight			Clear
I				▓	▓		E
N				▓			S
F		▓	▓				T
P				▓			J

Zimbabwean culture also is imaginative (N), conceptual (N), pressure-prompted (P), and open-ended (P).

Lesotho is ESFJ:

Clear				Slight			Clear
I				▓	▓		E
N				▓	▓	▓	S
F	▓	▓	▓				T
P				▓			J

Basotho culture also is quiet (I), casual (P) and open-ended (P).

Lesotho is on the tip of South Africa. "Basotho (People from Lesotho) get along smoothly with the most of the peoples of Southern Africa especially Botswana and Bapeli who are sometimes called Northern Basotho whilst we are known as Southern Basotho or just Bashoeshoe from the name of the founder of the Basotho nation, Moshoeshoe."

ASIA

Taiwan is ESFJ:

Clear				Slight			Clear
I				■			E
N				■	■		S
F		■	■				T
P				■			J

Taiwanese culture also is logical (T), pressure-prompted (P), and open-ended (P).

A female student from Taipei gave an extraverted feeling type description, "Taiwanese are kind, lazy, happy to talk to people and join groups." Another female Taiwanese said Taiwanese are tender yet ends-oriented; and reflective yet listen instead of read and write; and women are quiet and receiving.

Much like other introverted sensors they can have a bit of traditional mindset towards favoring males and the view of the roles men and women take. The SJ Taiwanese are serious about education, hardworking and hardsaving but they also know how to enjoy life. As ESFJs, Taiwanese love spectator sports like baseball and love going to the movies. They enjoy little appetizer foods and my ESFJ wife loves to death the little Taiwanese pineapple cake sold to tourists. Finding a country type similar to your own type may mean finding foods you love.

Malaysia is ESFJ:

Clear				Slight			Clear
I				▓			E
N				▓	▓		S
F		▓	▓				T
P				▓			J

A female student from Kuala Lumpur thought "people from Singapore, Brunei, and Hong Kong are similar to Malaysians." One man said, "Malaysians have a similarity to other people that lies somewhere between the Filipinos and Thais."

South Korea is ESFJ:

Clear				Slight			Clear
I				▓	▓	▓	E
N				▓	▓		S
F		▓	▓				T
P				▓			J

Korean culture also is original (N), reasonable (T), and pressure-prompted (P).

"Ethnologically, Koreans are quite similar to Mongolians and Japanese. Historically, Koreans have gotten along with Chinese." For the Koreans, as extraverted feeling types, personal relationships usually take priority over business.

Finding a country type similar to your type may mean finding TV that appeals to you. My ESFJ wife loves Korean television shows (dramas) and commercials. I speculate that even on the subconscious level there is an attraction to a culture that is the same type as your own. You will feel at ease yet not be able to explain why.

9

INFP—Introverted Feeling plus Extraverted Intuition

The next two chapters are about the introverted feeling mental process. INFPs and ISFPs prefer to use introverted feeling the majority of the time. Their second choice, in the case of the INFP would be extraverted intuition, and for the ISFP extraverted sensing.

Introverted Feeling vs Extraverted Feeling

My wife and I are both dominant feeling types—we lead with our feeling. This is a good match; we prefer to use feeling the majority of the time. This makes for good harmony, cooperation, a common interest and concern for people and society, and seeing the good and bad in people and society.

There also is another side to this equation, a complexity that has to be experienced firsthand like we have. I have some high ideals and my wife has coined some of my humanitarian plans for the world as 'Brentopia'. Bottom line is that she doesn't get it, both as a practical-minded sensing and an extraverted feeling type.

I lead with my favorite, introverted feeling, and she leads with her extraverted feeling. Her feeling is actualized in the outer world through taking action on the behalf of and for the benefit of others; also, through showing empathy and maintaining harmony with others. Some extraverts contend the outer world is the only real world.

My feeling is actuated in the inner world—which is just as real as the outer world. My feeling is expressed through my ideals, values, and beliefs. 'Brentopia' is a very real world within myself composed of all my hopes for humanity based on my personal understanding of universal truth.

For example, I know it to be true that all men should be treated equal and that includes work and pay too. Men are all of equal worth (some are NOT more equal than others) and therefore deserve the dignity of making the same amount of money for using their gifts, no matter what monetary value the world would like to assign to those gifts. One man's gifts are not worth less than another's. Therefore, compensation should be the same whether you are CEO or janitor, NBA star or writer, etc. Yes, this is the very 'real' inner world of the introverted feeling type that even the extraverted feeling type can't relate with and may even discount.

INFP— Introverted Feeling plus Extraverted Intuition

INFPs use introverted feeling and have a secondary preference for extraverted intuition. We all use introverted feeling when we depend on our inner value system to guide our actions and decisions. However, the INFP uses it more and is likely to be better at it than other types. Introverted feeling is what INFPs use in their inner, private world so it's difficult to observe in their actions or words. INFPs second preference is for extraverted intuition. Extraverted intuitive types explore new possibilities and form new ideas from the world around them. INFPs use extraverted intuition in the outer world and for interactions with others.

Introverted feeling can be contrasted with extraverted feeling in that it gets its values internally. For an introvert feeling type, an internal value system is developed and refined in accordance with their understanding and divining of universal truth. Extraverted feeling types values come from the community and people that surround them.

Introverted feeling types believe in the inherent good in everyone and altruism. The INFPsONLY Yahoo group had a religion poll and found one of the highest religions for INFPs was humanitarianism. I also selected humanitarianism as my religion because like many INFPs I believe in a higher ideal that goes beyond the limits of religion. INFPs love literature and communication through the written word. Their writing ability is intuition fueled by feeling. They can appear emotionless on the surface yet underneath feeling runs deep. Like an extraverted feeling type they desire loyalty, harmony and conflict-free relationships.

INFPs have an inner sense of other people's inner nature. One INTJ type expert said he envied the INFPs ability to see inside a person. INFPs get feeling impressions, tones and images of a person that make it seem like they can see inside a person. They perceive others intentions and motives through feeling tones. INFPs get a general feeling impression about a person, which is frequently accurate, yet they don't know why that person stimulated that impression within them. They somehow can sense the inner integrity of other people.

INFPs are mystical and soul connected. For me, my spiritual connection and knowing comes from my introverted feeling. I can sense something going on with others in my family. Japanese have a saying: *mushi ga shiraseru*—a little bug told me. For the introverted feeling type instead of information it's complex feeling tones. One day, when I was a teen, I had thoughts about my brother all morning. Later that day I found out he got a mild head concussion in gym class and lost his memory for a day. Other times I don't know who it is about. I just have an uneasy feeling. I sense something but can't put my finger on it until later I find out something was going on with one of my family members.

INFPs judge the world by their unique set of internal values and understand that everyone's values can be different. They can be passionate and enthusiastic about matters that relate to their personal values. They avoid the spotlight yet have inspirations and ideas they feel an urge to communicate—usually communicated in an introverted manner either in writing or one on one.

A country or culture of this type recognizes human potential and helps people actualize themselves. The culture is spiritually uplifting, optimistic and maintains high ideals. There is an atmosphere of seeking universal truth and an appreciation of aesthetics.

At worst these cultures can be highly judgmental; also, ignorant of the realities (physical, political) of the world around them. The dark side of this type is self-centeredness and an obsession with perfection and being a martyr or tyrant in service to its ideals.

INFP and ISFP have the same dominant function—introverted feeling. However, ENFP countries can be as appealing to INFP types as ISFP countries. ENFP and INFP countries have many similarities, like ENFP India and INFP Nepal.

Nepal is INFP and I am INFP. I heard a University of Hawaii (UH) professor from Nepal speak and read some of his research. I was surprised how much I connected with everything he said and wrote. It can be surprising the different ways and how easily a person can connect with other cultures and people from other cultures that are similar to his/her own type. My wife connects to ESFJ cultures in an introverted sensing and extraverted feeling way—spectator sports, TV, food, the kindness of people etc. As an INFP, I connect in an extraverted intuitive and introverted feeling way, such as research, ideas, religion, etc.

The third and fourth mental processes of the INFP are extraverted sensing and extraverted thinking. This is the weak spot of the INFPs. As an INFP, living in the extraverted sensing culture of ESFP Hawaii drives me nuts with its rivalry, and lack of judgment. Growing up in ESTJ American culture drove me nuts with its extraverted thinking insensitivity. I tend to project a lot of negative stuff onto these cultures as a result of them being my weak spot. So to get out of the negative aspects of my third and fourth mental processes I allow them to be expressed occasionally by doing some sensory play, tending the yard, organizing something, or technical computer work.

On the other hand, my seventh and eighth mental processes are introverted sensing and introverted thinking. I am attracted to introverted thinking like INTP author David Keirsey's book *Please Understand Me II*. I understand it but don't have that introverted thinker ability to name something for what it is, properly classify and assign it its proper place. I admire introverted thinking because it's so foreign to my natural ability of introverted feeling. Also, the introverted sensing of the ISFJ Japanese has also always been a mystery to me. Yet, I admire the introverted sensors photographic memory, their attachment to the past and ability to fully relive a past sensation or experience.

ASIA

Nepal is INFP:

Clear			Slight			Clear
I			▓▓			E
N		▓▓	▓▓			S
F	▓▓	▓▓	▓▓			T
P		▓▓	▓▓			J

Nepali culture also is active (E), traditional (S), and early start-ing (J). (The end of Chapter 2 has a decription of each facet.)

Nepal is a Hindu country. Hindus constitute 80.6% of the population. Buddhists make up 10.7%, Muslims 4.2%, Kirant 3.6%, other religions 0.9%. There is an intermingling of Hindu and Buddhist beliefs in Nepal. They share temples and worship common deities. Throughout history it has been a land of religious harmony. Its neighbors, ESFP Tibet and ENFP India, influence Nepal's culture.

One Hindu Nepali said, "The birthplace of Buddha is in Nepal." INFPs are seen as missionaries, ministers and priests so it isn't surprising that the birthplace of Buddha is an INFP country. One person reported Mongolia as INFP, which also isn't surpris-ing because they are Tibetan Buddhist and gave the Dalai Lama his name. Another person reported INFP for the birthplace of Mahatma Gandhi (Gujarat, India). Lastly, one person from Chuuk (Federated States of Micronesia) reported INFP, however, Chuuk is ISFP.

"Nepal is most similar to Thailand. Nepali are unique, tolerant, friendly and reserved"—sort of an INFP in a nutshell. "Men are more expressive but women are more controlled." He said, "Nepalis operate by crisis management. If they have a whole month to get something done they wait until the last five days to get it done"—a classic perceiving type.

Search the Internet for what 'Nepalis are known for' and find INFP looking descriptions. Nepalis are known for: their social good-will, harmony and mutual tolerance, courage and bravery, skill and endurance in the face of danger, visits all over the world and greater liberalism of both action and views on religion. Nepalis are NOT known for destruction, vandalism. Even the dark side of the INFP is mentioned, " Nepalis are known for their conspiracy theories because nobody bothers filling them in on what's going on."

Burma (Myanmar) is INFP:

Clear   Slight   Clear

I			▓				E
N			▓				S
F	▓	▓	▓				T
P			▓				J

Burmese culture also is gregarious (E), active (E), realistic (S), traditional (S), systematic (T), methodical (J).

The same group of languages is spoken in various central and south Asian countries, including Myanmar, northern Thailand, western, central and southern China (Tibet), Nepal, Bhutan, India, and western Pakistan. There is a commonality between INFP Burma and INFP Nepal through language and religion.

I met one UH student from Yangon (Rangoon). She said, "Burmese aren't outgoing like the Thais. Burmese are similar to Cambodians and Laotians but not the Vietnamese who are more hard working and assertive."

10

ISFP—Introverted Feeling plus Extraverted Sensing

ISFPs use introverted feeling and have a secondary preference for extraverted sensing. We all use introverted feeling when we depend on our inner value system to guide our actions and decisions. However, the ISFP uses it more and is likely to be better at it than other types. Introverted feeling is what ISFPs use in their inner, private world so it's difficult to observe in their actions or words. ISFPs second preference is for is extraverted sensing. Extraverted sensing types engage all five senses, spontaneously interact with the world and live fully in the moment. ISFPs use extraverted sensing in the outer world and for interactions with others.

Both ISFP and INFP have a dominant feeling process that is introverted. The ISFP expresses introverted feeling in the outside world through sensing actions—they are practical helpers. It is hard to tell what the introverted feeling types' inner values are because they come out in sometimes awkward sensing actions or intuitive thoughts and words. They selectively choose the sensing actions and intuitive thoughts that they think represent their inner values. Inner values that are sometimes not even clear to them can seem even more confusing to others.

Both types are easy going and adaptable and very loyal but like all types can also have a dark side under distress. The weakness of an introvert is a lack of information about the outside world. Under stress the ISFP may rely on learned stereotypes and the INFP may have theories of others conspiring.

In introvert societies values are not written on the wall. People coming in have to really make an effort to bridge an understanding. In an ISFP society actions more than words convey peoples inner values. It is up to the outsider to try to interpret what those values are from watching the actions of the locals and the interactions they experience with the locals.

ASIA

Cambodia is ISFP:

Clear				Slight			Clear
I			▓				E
N				▓	▓		S
F	▓	▓					T
P		▓	▓				J

Cambodian culture also is gregarious (E), expressive (E), abstract (N), and early starting (J). (The end of Chapter 2 has a decription of each facet.)

Cambodians are Theravada Buddhist. Theravada (literally, "the Way of the Elders") is the oldest surviving Buddhist school, and for many centuries has been the religion of Cambodia, Laos, Myanmar, Malaysia, Indonesia, Thailand, Sri Lanka, and parts of southwest China. Theravada Buddhist countries tend to be introverted feeling: Cambodia is ISFP, Sri Lanka and Thailand are ESFP, and the majority of China is ISFP.

Cambodians as introverted feeling types don't show their emotions in public. One Cambodian UH graduate said, "Outside, Cambodians don't show it but inside they feel resentment against the Vietnamese. The Vietnamese liberation force (liberation from the Khmer Rouge) put a Vietnam-friendly government in place. With the Vietnamese, we are willing to forgive, put it aside and move forward but we keep losing pieces of land to Vietnam." They can't start the healing process because they are losing land. This sounds like introverted feeling types desire for healing.

"Cambodians are open-minded, peace-seeking, reserved and private." They are perceiving types and are comfortable with being informal. For example, they wear clothing similar to pajamas as daily wear. "They are very casual you don't have to call to visit, you can just show up and eat lunch if its lunch time or whatever is available if its not mealtime, and sit around and talk."

China is ISFP:

Clear				Slight			Clear
I		▓	▓				E
N				▓	▓		S
F	▓	▓	▓				T
P		▓	▓				J

Chinese culture also is gregarious (E), abstract (N), and scheduled (J).

Han Chinese constitute about 91.9% of the total population of China and are the largest single human ethnic group in the world, numbering over 1.3 billion people. The Han Chinese have sixteen major dialects (which are associated with one or more provinces (33 in total) or municipalities (4 in total). However, I found dividing by dialects doesn't makes any difference in type. Also, dividing by religion isn't feasible. Half the population is atheist and the largest religious group is about 100 million Buddhists (6% of the population). I divided China by provinces. The majority are ISFP and are located along the east coast (where the majority of the population is).

Provinces

Hebei (north coast)—ISFP

Zhejiang (west coast)- ISFP

Guangdong (south coast)- ISFP

Yunnan (southwest bordering INFP Burma)- ENFJ

Municipalities

Bejing (north)—ESTP

Chongqing (west central)—ESFP

One Tibetan student said, "On Chinese websites there are always debates between Christians and non-Christians. The Chinese have to honor their ancestors, yet Christianity says you will not go to heaven unless you are saved. Therefore, a Chinese-Christian will not meet his ancestors in the afterlife." This is a problem for Chinese-Christians because ancestor worship is a strong, long-standing belief in China. If they are Christian they cannot worship their ancestors and their descendants cannot worship them. Their dead ancestors are condemned to roam eternity as lonely, hungry ghosts.

I interviewed a female UH student that was a Han Chinese from the Yunnan Province of China. Yunnan is in southern China on the border of Myanmar, Laos and Vietnam. She compared meeting people for the first time in the USA to China. Chinese are introverted and feeling types. "Americans look friendly and happy but Chinese are more calm and quiet but become easy going when they find that person is nice. Americans also tend to forget others easily even after being friendly with them. Chinese friends don't care about money. When going out, they pay for their friends." Chinese are loyal, value harmony and avoiding bringing shame to others. "Americans can criticize everything about another person but Chinese cannot unless they are close friends. It's not right for me to say something bad about China or Chinese." She felt she has to protect the reputation of her country.

She felt Asians in general are more feeling. A female Vietnamese student also made the same comment. In class students from Asian cultures (such as India, China, Korea, and even Iraq) give an opposite opinion but Americans give criticism. "When critiquing a term paper Asians say 'these things are good but if you do this and this it will be better', but Americans just say the paper is bad."

In one class a professor asked all the students to comment about several pictures from different countries (Asia, Hawaii, America, etc). "Asians always said something good about the pictures but Americans always said something insensitive that hurt the Asian students." She is frequently hurt because American classmates make comments about China and don't consider her feelings. This

sounds like an introverted feeling type that can have turmoil of emotion inside but appear calm on the outside, so Americans don't realize she is offended.

There are also things she doesn't like about her own culture. "I want to keep something a secret—but I get comments and judgments from the people around me." She feels she doesn't have a right to follow her own ideas that she has to follow their advice. When she makes a decision she has to consider a lot of people and a lot of different aspects. She feels this might lead her to make the wrong decision like in marriage, etc. "Also, if they give me too much attention or more care I feel more stressful. I cannot be independent because it's the Chinese culture." She feels some don't really want to help her. "They just want to criticize my private business."

She feels, "Americans as individualists have more space to develop their abilities and freedom of choice. For example, when Chinese choose a university they have to consider what relatives and friends think, also whether it has job prospects, and whether it is a famous university."

She likes the judging aspects of Chinese culture. Chinese have an introverted sensing (SJ) work ethic. "The Chinese are so hard-working because of population pressure and the competition is so intense." Another student said being practical (sensing) is preferred by modern Chinese and conceptual (intuition) is valued by old Chinese. Chinese are questioning (thinking) of people with lower status and accommodating (feeling) to peers and people with higher status.

"The western part of China has the most ethnic groups and the culture is more colorful and friendlier. The western part has more original Chinese language usage. Because of poor transportation ethnics tend to stay in their groups but when going to the cities they don't. Confucius is from Shandong province (on the north coast), this may be the most classic ethnic Chinese area."

OCEANIA

Federated States of Micronesia (including Republic of Palau, Chuuk, and Kosrae) are ISFP:

Clear				Slight			Clear
I							E
N							S
F							T
P							J

Palauan people as introverted feeling types have core values and seek harmony. In the University of Hawaii East-West Center dormitories, the bathrooms have shower stalls. There is only one bathroom on each floor so both men and women share the bathroom. The toilets have doors but the shower stalls have smaller doors where you can still see a person's head and feet.

This might be inconsiderate to women in American culture, however, one Palauan lady felt that this was disrespectful to the guys because in her culture the men are to be respected. "Palau is a maternal society but we respect men." One lady from Kosrae said, "you have to be mindful when you do things. People look at your family not only you. You can get labeled."

"We make people feel welcome if they come to our country. We like to have kinship and we stick together as a group when abroad." There were four of them sitting in the front lounge of the East West Center together. Two from Chuuk, one from Palau and one from Marshall Islands. The Palauan only spoke Palauan and English. The one from the Marshall Islands spoke Marshallese and English. "When we are together we speak English because it is the common language for all of us" even though they are all Micronesians.

EUROPE

Andorra is ISFP:

Clear				Slight				Clear
I	▓	▓	▓					E
N				▓	▓	▓		S
F		▓						T
P		▓						J

Andorran culture also is tough (T).

Andorra is a small, landlocked principality in south-western Europe, located in the eastern Pyrenees Mountains and bordered by France and Spain. The country's population is 68,403: Spanish (43%), Andorran (33%), Portuguese (11%), French (7%), and others (6%).

Lichtenstein is ISFP:

Clear			Slight			Clear
I		▓	▓				E
N				▓	▓	▓	S
F			▓				T
P			▓				J

Lichtenstein culture also is active (E), empathic (F), tender (F), systematic (J), and scheduled (J).

Slovakia is ISFP:

Clear			Slight			Clear
I		▓	▓				E
N				▓			S
F		▓	▓				T
P			▓				J

Slovak culture also is enthusiastic (E), abstract (N), imaginative (N), reasonable (T), scheduled (J), and methodical (J).

11

ENFP—Extraverted Intuition plus Introverted Feeling

The next two chapters are about the extraverted intuition mental process. ENFPs and ENTPs prefer to use extraverted intuition the majority of the time. Their second choice, in the case of the ENFP, would be introverted feeling, and for the ENTP, introverted thinking.

Extraverted intuitive types can see ideas springing from ideas right in front of their eyes. They see so many possibilities for things out in the real world and real world situations that are overflowing with potential. Their intuition focuses on the outside world and they can see the future possibilities, especially in their areas of expertise. For an ENFP their interest may not lie in business or technology (like an ENTP) but instead people concerns.

Intuitive types look to the future whereas introverted sensors look to the past. As an extraverted intuitive, I get a sort of reverse nostalgia through future associations. My daughter can fit her whole body in my pajama pants bottoms and its sad to think about the day when she won't do stuff like that and couldn't fit in them anyway. My introverted sensing wife does past associations for nostalgia with both things and feelings. The introverted sensing Japanese actually have two separate words for these two types of nostalgia. More words in language is an indicator of preferences.

ENFPs use extraverted intuition and have a secondary preference for introverted feeling. We all use extraverted intuition when
we explore new possibilities and form new ideas from the world
around us. However, the ENFP uses it more and is likely to be better
at it than other types. Extraverted intuition is what ENFPs use in
the outer world and with interactions with others. ENFPs second
preference is for introverted feeling. Introverted feeling types have a
complex inner value system that guides their actions and decisions.
ENFPs use introverted feeling in their inner, private world so it's
difficult to observe in their actions or words.

EURASIA

Russia is ENFP:

Clear				Slight			Clear
I				▓	▓	▓	E
N	▓	▓	▓				S
F	▓	▓	▓				T
P			▓				J

Russian culture also is experiential (S) and early-starting (J).
(The end of Chapter 2 has a decription of each facet.)

I asked one Russian in Slovakia if I should divide Russia up
by regional differences because it is so large. They replied, "Please,
don't divide Russia! There are many other people who want to do
this. And if serious, you'd better study culture from inside the culture. Visit different places and towns of Russia, speak to people,
try to accept their 'world picture—it is revealed everywhere, in some
words, opinions, beliefs, etc. Of course, you will meet different people—some will give you the only piece of bread they have, others will
not want to speak to you. You see, these people you can meet even
in one and the same village, and suppose, there are different styles
and cultures and more than 100 peoples in Russia. The mode of
life in Tatarstan or Kalmykia is very different from the mode of life
in Zabajkalje, for example, or in Korjakija. And if you take megapo-
lices, such as Moscow you will not get an understandable picture. It
is as Babylon—many peoples, cultures, traditions all in one."

Intuitive feeling types base their decisions on information supplied by intuition and complex inner feeling tones. She gave this intuitive feeling answer to the study of Russian culture: "If your task (so hard a task) is to understand the main cultural models of different countries, I suppose, you are going to have to live in the country a minimum of a month, communicating with different people and then construct your own impression. Don't try to realize. Don't use your mental facilities. It is in vain. Listen to your heart, by your heart, collect your impressions—your soul-work, not mind-work. That will be more resulting. Feel and penetrate on the 'thin' plan. Otherwise you will not succeed (to the great expend, because of the lack of time). You know, to do things well is very difficult, even to clean streets. "

"I'm sure a person has to know the language (the type of language, the mode of motivation of words, the list of marked out notions—everything gives you deep, inside information about peoples), to live among these people, to breathe that air, to enjoy their food (tell me what you're eating and I'll tell you what you are), to have fun with them, to be troubled with them—as we say, 'to eat a pound of salt with them' (in Russian, 'pud'=16 kg)."

According to Craig Storti in his book *Cross-Cultural Dialogues*, "Russians believe that happiness is no more the norm than sadness or depression, that each is a natural and inevitable part of life, and that one is just as likely to occur as the other." They don't feel a need to fix someone's sadness or depression. Russian "instinct is to not act but to cope. Why this American insistence on being happy? It probably relates to our belief in the power of individuals to shape events and control their own destinies." Storti gives the example of The Declaration of Independence having the pursuit of happiness as an inalienable right.

UH Professor of Psychology Julia Nikulina Compton (who is from Russia) commented at the 1998 Psychological Type and Culture Conference, "Although Americans are kind of emotional and happy; it doesn't go very deep from the Russian perspective. You have to be much more emotional, and you have to show your real soul. In Russia there's a big emphasis on feeling and intuition.

This is something that is very valued by society and people are supposed to keep that script. A lot of foreigners who are not familiar with Russian culture are viewed as cold and distant."

She gave a personal example of where the Russian soul was seen, "after several hours of drinking and socializing, all the people started pouring out their souls to each other...men kissing and hugging and declaring that they are friends forever. From the Russian point of view, this is normal behavior and they were just following the script. That's the way you open up to others. There is a great value on openness and emotionality...emotional and spontaneous and strong emotions are valued." Russian value feeling over thinking, there is a saying: "the soul doesn't operate on logic". Throughout Russian history humor has been an expression of the human spirit.

Communication Gap

You can find out the types that have the hardest time communicating by switching the middle two letters of the type (e.g. ENFP becomes ESTP). These two types have to use their least developed mental processes to communicate with each other. The communication gap is the hardest to bridge between types that have the two middle letters opposite. The opposite for ENFP Russians is ESTP but ESTJ also is a large communication gap and this may be why the ENFP Russians have had communication barriers with ESTJ Americans.

Georgia is ENFP:

Clear				Slight				Clear
I				▓	▓	▓		E
N			▓					S
F	▓	▓	▓					T
P	▓	▓	▓					J

Georgian culture also is receiving (I) and traditional (S).

CENTRAL ASIA

Mongolia is ENFP:

Clear				Slight			Clear
I				■			E
N			■				S
F		■	■				T
P	■	■	■				J

Mongolian culture also is intimate (I), quiet (I), practical (S), traditional (S), and reasoning (T).

Central Asia has historically been closely tied to its nomadic peoples and the Silk Road. Mongolia's population is about 2.6 million. The culture of Mongolia can be described as homogeneous. 96% of Mongolia's population is Vajrayana Buddhist in the Tibetan tradition. In the 16th century the Mongolian leader gave the name Dalai Lama to the visiting head of the Tibetan Buddhism and it has been used ever since. Dalai Lama means "ocean of wisdom" in Mongolian. (*Wikipedia*)

Many Mongols describe themselves as quiet and traditional. One commented, "Mongols introduce people, seek popularity and want contact with others. Most of the city people are sociable but the herdsmen are reserved." They are practical in all areas of life and trust experience. Most Mongolians are accepting and trusting as a result of the deep-rooted influence of Buddhism. Most of the Mongolians in the rural area are means-oriented as a result of a nomadic life. "The education system is motivated by pressure because the influence of the old centralized system is still there."

Kyrgyzstan is ENFP:

Clear				Slight			Clear
I				▓	▓		E
N			▓				S
F	▓	▓	▓				T
P	▓	▓	▓				J

Kyrgyz culture also is quiet (I) and traditional (S) (both like Mongolia) plus experiential (S).

Kyrgyzstan is a Central Asian country with both eastern and western features. Landlocked and mountainous it is known as "Switzerland of Central Asia". They are a bilingual society speaking both Russian and Kyrgyz. "Under the Soviet Union their culture wasn't destroyed but suppressed and preserved underground. They have had difficulties implementing the capitalist system since they became an independent sovereign state from the Soviet Union in 1991"—sounds like an NFP culture trying to implement an STJ system. Last year they had a revolution. "It was more a revolution between political parties than a revolution of the people."

I interviewed a UH East-West Center student who is an ISFJ and reported Kyrgyzstan as an ENFP culture. In Kyrgyzstan, two thirds of the population live in rural areas but she is from the city and looks of Eastern Asian descent. She said, "Kyrgyz women are not subservient like Eastern Asian women." She is from the city but felt the country values were the true Kyrgyz. She is an SJ who looks fondly on the traditional values yet has regrets that her country isn't more westernized.

Kyrgyz people are perceiving types. She described them as relaxed, careless, lazy and not energetic. She gave me an example from a Kyrgyz legend: "At the beginning of mankind, God gave land to every people, according to their talents and personality. He distributed fertile valleys, rocky mountains, dry deserts, forests, and everything the world had to offer. At the end of the distribution, God noticed the Kyrgyz, who had been sleeping at the foot of a tree, when everybody else was fighting for the best part of the world.

This carelessness touched God so much in his very heart, that he decided to give him an especially fertile and beautiful part of the world, so he wouldn't have to work too hard to survive."

They prefer extroversion but also the quiet facet. "Kyrgyz are patient, calm, quiet, they wait and give you time—much more than Americans" This is the accommodating characteristic of feeling. "Conversation is more casual than in America but not as long pauses as in Japan." Their extroversion and feeling preferences can be seen in their weddings. "At a Kyrgyz wedding there are many long toasts and people sing as a gift to the wedding couple. Yr-kese means song bowl. At births or other celebrations we pass the bowl and the person holding it sings a song."

She sees the need for her country to become more like the west yet she wonders at its obsession with the Russian language education system. "We apply western values to academic achievement and financial independence. We believe a Russian language education is going to be more strict and demanding which Kyrgyz feel they need because this is the opposite of their culture. They believe your going to get more knowledge in a Russian school. The Kyrgyz section of schools are always less equipped—they have smaller rooms and less equipment."

"Kyrgyz feel Russian speaking professionals are more competent and believe the Russian system was very good especially in science. There is no university level education in the Kyrgyz language but we have Turkish and English (at the American University in Central Asia). We try to learn English and computer skills because of better jobs and opportunities."

They are intuitive but still prefer the sensing facet of tradition. Their traditions and language were lost while part of the Soviet Union. "I speak more Russian than Kyrgyz and not all the public schools teach in Kyrgyz—more teach in Russian. Traditional ways still prevail. We respect old people and follow their advice. Old people have life experience: they are expected to know and understand life better. Sometimes parents still arrange marriages. Parents aren't supposed to live alone when they get old. The youngest son has the responsibility to take care of them."

They respect age and higher position. "You can't call an older person or person in a higher position by first name. It has to be the formal. In the office, you call them by their first and middle name. Or outside the office you call *baike* (aunt, uncle) to anyone who is older. This is kind of like man or sir in English. Despite this we are not in general very official."

"We are not very religious but religion serves a traditional function. Kyrgyz are liberal Muslims who follow some basic principles of Islam. Basic holidays and traditions; burial and birth rituals are according to Islamic ways. The majority of people don't pray (typical Muslims pray five times a day). Kyrgyz used to be part of the Soviet Union and religion was not allowed."

There are feeling values seen in marriage. "There are no boundaries between wife and husband. Kyrgyz are very dependent on each other. In a marriage there is no separate bank accounts for a husband and wife. They are more tolerant of each other. There are no marriage agreements. That would be weird because that is like a thinking type—thinking about the money. We are very dependant on family, relatives and friends. Divorce is not a good thing, and they keep marriage together if at the least for children."

Although intuitive, they value tradition (sensing) in marriage. "Men and women have certain jobs and emotions. Women are supposed to be more emotional. They have a saying that the man is the head but the wife is the neck. Where the neck will turn the head will look in that direction. Women try to make men think they are the head and decide everything. Women also take positions of leadership. However, they want the man to lead and take the positions of leadership, but women still want the control."

Kyrgyz living abroad experience type clashes. "Many Kyrgyz people move to Russia and Germany and find they can't fit in so they move back. It is because of Eastern values that are in Kyrgyzstan but not in those countries. Oriental values of being more open, hospitable, friendly, talkative, etc." The feeling type Kyrgyz have trouble with thinking western culture.

"Many Germans that grew up in Kyrgyzstan emigrated to Germany but later moved back to Kyrgyzstan. They said it was difficult for them to communicate in Germany. Things like you need to call before visiting in Germany. In Kyrgyzstan it is more casual you can just drop by and visit without notice. Also, when people invite others to visit they expect them to be late so if they want them to arrive at 5pm they will tell people to come at 4pm."

India is ENFP:

Clear				Slight			Clear
I				▓			E
N			▓				S
F		▓	▓				T
P		▓	▓				J

Indian culture also is contained (I), intimate (I), realistic (S), traditional (S), reasonable (T), scheduled (J).

\India is definitely a microcosm of the world as a whole, with different regions reporting different types. Like China I have broken up India by regions and states. There are 35 states but I only have a typed a few of them. There are obvious differences between regions and I felt it necessary to divide India considering the population is over a billion.

"As far as India is concerned it's really complex. Each state is a different region and we see a lot of difference in people (food, worship, caste, language, wardrobe) so if you take Hindus, for example, are not the same throughout the country, even the worship rites change. I really think you will not be able to cover the entire India unless you cover it by state."

Indians are extraverts. "If you talk to an Indian from your heart, he/she will open the book of his/her life in next 10 minutes conversation. There is nothing personal in their life. They need no space from their parents, brother or sister, so they are expressive and easier to know! You don't see an abyss deep in their mind. It's like 30 feet of the Pacific Ocean you can see everything clearly from top and everything is clear." As I have seen with some other Asian countries the quiet facet seems to be associated with women. "The reserved character (quiet, serene) is admired for women but for men they want to see a active gregarious person. So we are breaking out of the shell but this is still exists."

Indians are intuitive yet traditional. "They are not that much innovative. They try to follow the stepping stone which is built by their father, grandfather or may be which has been built from their ancestors or what they are seeing around them."

Indians are feeling types. "I strongly agree with this. India follows 'unity in diversity'. They are generally less arguable and tend to be more agreeable with one's opinion. They believe in peace. More than 40 countries have attacked India and this country has never started a war against any country unless they had been provoked! They live in harmony and peace. There are tons of different religions, languages and dialects but still it stands united. If you travel from north to south India, you can literally see the two different

worlds together!" Indians are feeling types, yet reasonable and firm. "It's hard to divert an Indian from his path because they are just firm-minded."

One female UH student surprised me when she answered ENTP for India because India is so spiritual and religious I expected NF. She said, "It is logical to be spiritual in India." She is from the south and the ENTP type fits the technologically advanced area in southern India, south of Bombay/Mumbai and Hyderabad.

A male UH student from Gujarat (the state above Bombay) said, "India is a mélange. The south is very traditional but admired for their intelligence and technology. They follow tradition—yet at the same time keep up with technology. The north is stereotyped as adventurous, shrewd and clever." Another student said, "Northern Indians (Punjabi, Gujarati) are the businessmen seen in the USA, UK and Africa." One Indian friend commented "the Gujaratis own many taxis, motels and convenience stores in the USA." Some of these stereotypes are seen in American television shows like The Simpsons where an Indian named Apu is a convenience store owner. Also, in the American movie "Mississippi Masala" the Indian family owns a motel. Perhaps because of this relative success, Gujaratis are racially stereotyped as being hard working and frugal.

Also, one UH student reported Gujarat as INFP. Gujarat is the birthplace of Mahatma Gandhi. This interesting because INFPs are idealist (many are religious) and willing to sacrifice for what they believe in and even sometimes seen as martyrs—similar to Gandhi.

Another guy from Kerlala (the state on the southwestern tip of India) reported ENFP. His area is Hindu (40%), Christian (25%), Muslim (25%) with 100% literacy rate and good healthcare. He said, "There is a huge gap between the north and south. The south is better educated and economically better off. The Indians from Hyderabad are academically ahead and seen in American Universities and the IT sector (like Silicon Valley). I heard that 28% of NASA is South Indians."

The faith of more than 80.4% of the people is Hinduism, considered the world's oldest religious and philosophical system. Islam is practiced by around 13.4% of all Indians and Christianity is

2.3%. Based on responses I speculate the southern Indian Hindus are ENFP and the northern Indian Hindus are INFP (like the Nepal Hindus), the Indian Muslims are ESFP (like Pakistan), and the Christians (Tamils) in India are ISFJ. One of the stereotypes on the internet for Indians is the "ability to fit in anywhere in the world". According to one type expert ENFPs have the easiest time adjusting to other cultures.

The overall consensus or average was ENFP:

Tamil Nadu (Southeast tip of India) is ISFJ (Christian Tamils)

Kerlala (Southwest tip of India) is ENFP

South is ENFP

Hyderabad is ENTP

Gujarati (Western tip) is INFP

Punjabi (Northern area) ESFP

EUROPE

Bulgaria is ENFP:

Clear				Slight			Clear
I				▓	▓	▓	E
N			▓				S
F			▓				T
P		▓	▓				J

Bulgarian culture also is critical (T).

One HPU student from the capital city of Sofia felt, "Bulgarians are exactly the same as their neighbors the Macedonians and Serbians. Bulgarians are systematic as a result of the previous communism. Yet they are not scheduled like Americans and are spontaneous." Another person summed up Bulgarians as "initiating, expressive and casual."

Italy is ENFP:

Clear				Slight			Clear
I				▓	▓	▓	E
N			▓				S
F			▓				T
P	▓	▓	▓				J

Italian culture also is experiential (S), concrete (S), questioning (T), and critical (T).

Denmark is ENFP:

Clear				Slight			Clear
I				▓			E
N			▓				S
F			▓				T
P			▓				J

Danish culture also is intimate (I) and experiential (S).

"It's really hard to describe the character of the Danish people in general, as the diversity is great and character further differentiates with geography and urbanite." Denmark was split between the University of Hawaii students reporting ENFP the foreign embassies reporting ESTJ. A small German-speaking minority lives in southern part of Denmark—could this be the reason for the ESTJs?

One friendly, helpful Danish guy said the Danish get their imaginative side from the Arctic school. The northern part of Greenland (in the Arctic circle) also is ENFP like Denmark and they share this imaginative facet (Greenland is part of Denmark—see the ENFJ Greenland country profile). Maybe the ESTJ represents the urbanite and the university students the Artic school?

He said Danish are like ESTJ Americans rooting for the little man, the underdog against the system, but they are not as systematic as the ISTJ Germans. They also have ESTJ neighbors in the Netherlands and England. The embassy gave me a Danish government publication on globalization, which read very ESTJ with concerns over being competitive and productivity growth.

He said they think of themselves as the Italians (the Italians are also ENFP) of Scandinavian countries, and like many small countries want to differentiate themselves from the countries around them. This sounds like an ENFP description: "In general all Danish people are cozy and cheerful. We like to have a nice time with our family and friends." Also, an example of the extraverted intuitive Danish looking to the future: "The Danish Government has engaged wholeheartedly in preparing Denmark for an increasingly globalized world and this process has now caught the attention of many governments, who want to learn from this."

Ireland is ENFP:

Clear				Slight			Clear
I				▓	▓	▓	E
N			▓				S
F	▓	▓	▓				T
P	▓	▓	▓				J

Irish culture also is experiential (S) and traditional (S).

The Irish are clearly extraverts. "Irish people tend to be chatty and are good with small talk, especially in situations where they don't know anyone. Irish people tend to joke about themselves more, so you get to know a bit about the person, especially in a pub or social setting." Being gregarious "depends more on the individual, but it is more accepted that you have a broad circle of friends and are popular, loners tend to be stigmatized. I think Irish people like to chat and find out about each other's news, people stop to chat to each other on the street, and if you are out for a walk and pass strangers you tend to greet them."

As extraverted intuitive types Irish favor abstraction and being intellectual. "Even though people like chatting and finding out each other's news, they may not give away too many secrets and may talk vaguely about things rather than giving away the facts." For the "Irish yes is maybe and no is yes. I would say that Irish people are

generally well educated and come up with ideas, may not always be good ones though!"

The Irish also prefer sensing traditionalism. "Generally people tend to be conservative and don't want to stick out as being too radical, they do things the way things always have been done, but once a new way of doing things comes along, they adapt quickly, e.g. smoking ban in pubs." The Irish have only a slight preference for intuition and sometimes show their ESFP side. "Irish people like *craic* (Irish word for fun) and having a good time, which usually involves a few drinks, too."

They have a clear secondary preference for introverted feeling. For example they can be accommodating: "Irish people don't want to rock the boat too much, they may even pretend that things are okay even though they are not, e.g. if someone is quite ill, they may say that they are fine." The Irish have an NF idealism: they were one of the first EU nations to open their doors to immigrants from Eastern Europe (e.g. Poland) to work and live in Ireland.

The Irish have a clear perceiving preference for being casual, open-ended and spontaneous. "People tend to be easy going, perhaps they were more so years ago before the price increases and high inflation. They definitely are more go with the flow people, if they make plans they do not necessarily divulge them to other people, they see what happens and don't book up their weekends months in advance, tend not to have diaries but this depends on the individual. Irish people don't tend to plan their social life weeks in advance, you can go to the pub any night, and don't need a reason for doing so. They generally like to meet new people."

Spain is ENFP:

Clear				Slight			Clear
I							E
N							S
F							T
P							J

Spanish culture is experiential (S) and questioning (T).

One Spainard said, "bear in mind that Spain is made up of very different regions (they want to be called 'nations' lately) and the customs, character of people and so on tend to be quite different from one another. Please, keep in mind that there are very marked differences between Andalucians in the South and Galicians, Basques, etc in the North and Catalonians in the East and Castilians in the center."

"If one wanted to categorize about the qualities and characteristics of the Spanish people, perhaps a division along the lines of North and South may provide a more realistic description of the characters of people inhabiting Spain. If one were to stereotype a bit, one could say that the farther South in Spain one goes, the more people are extraverted, open, fun loving, spontaneous, explosive, emotional, outspoken, fast thinking, very reactive to things.

Going further towards the North people tend to be considerably more reserved, introverted, cautious, suspicious, methodical, down to earth, not prone to high states of excitation, more conservative, less experimental. "

The Spanish are clearly extraverts. "On the average, Spanish people are very open and prone to establish social contacts very effortlessly and naturally. They thrive on social interaction and in general are very outgoing people, extraverted and open to strangers. These characteristics are easily observed in the interaction of people in the ubiquitous bars and cafes. The Spaniard is a gregarious person almost by definition. They like groups, they like social interaction in large groups, they enjoy eating together, which can become a very elaborate social act and seek the companionship of others readily and instinctively. The Spaniard tends to be dramatic, emotional, with easy colloquial conversation, humour is an inseparable part of the interaction among people, descriptions of events are lively and graphical, dramatization and hand/body language are very much part of their way of socially interacting."

Extroversion differs across regions of Spain. "People in the South of Spain are considerably more easy to know than people in the North. The northerner, specially Galicians are more introspective, more cautious and don't open up as easily to strangers or even people they know." Also, in terms of wanting contact and interaction, "there is definitely a difference between Northerners and Southerners. In general, however, the typical Spanish person likes social interaction, visiting and being visited at home, meeting people for all kinds of activities, conversation and good humour flows easily. Conversations tend to be loud, with people generally competing for the last word, there is even physical contact and not as much of a need for personal space or for privacy as in other cultures."

Spanish have a preference for intuition. "In general, the Spanish people are very fond of abstract discussions and elaborate argumentation to make and win a point. Reading the press or listening to many of the radio or TV programs give an indication for their fondness of intellectual discussion and intricate argumentation. The reasoning and mental ability for discussion of the average Spanish person is always a pleasant surprise to me. You find intellectual interest among people that one wouldn't expect and at levels of intensity that would surprise most people." Another example of intuitive resourcefulness: "While the Dutch live surrounded by water, the Spaniards have problems to collecting it. That is why the cunning Spaniards developed a very interesting way to collect it. Their roofs are used to collect rain water that flows directly to a well below the basement (called in Spanish *algibe*). In that manner they had always fresh water. The well itself also refreshed the whole house." The one exception to their preference for intuition is that they trust their experience. "The Spaniard is eminently sensual and trusts and relies more on the information coming from his senses than the deductions and theoretical elucidations of other cultures."

The Spanish have a slight preference for feeling especially being empathic and compassionate. "A quality of the Spanish people is to empathize with other people misfortunes and being able to put themselves in other people's shoes." The Spanish are truly balanced between feeling and thinking. For example, they can be both critical and accepting. Also, the Spanish show their thinking side by being challenging and wanting discussion. Like a classic ENTP type (the type the Spanish would be if they had a thinking preference) "the Spaniard treats discussion, even argumentations almost like a sport and an end in itself."

Spanish have a very clear preference for perceiving. "Organizational skills are not the main quality of Spanish people who tend to be impetuous, spontaneous and correct after the fact rather than plan ahead to prevent problems. Spanish people get easily tired of routine and need stimulation, whether intellectual or otherwise. They tend to be very spontaneous in their behaviour, not good planners, or good examiners of issues ahead of time. They tend to jump in head first. A Spanish person is predominantly unpredictable, spontaneous and a bit non-conformist."

LATIN AMERICA

Belize is ENFP:

Clear				Slight			Clear
I				▓			E
N			▓	▓			S
F		▓	▓				T
P			▓				J

Belizean culture also is intimate (I), quiet (I), concrete (S), realistic (S), questioning (T), early starting (J), and scheduled (J).

One Belizean gave festival preparations as a pressure-prompted example of perceiving. Concerning "the Festival of la Costa Maya. I am not from San Pedro, but sometimes we feel that nothing is being done, but at the end everything comes out alright."

Honduras is ENFP:

Clear				Slight			Clear
I				▓	▓	▓	E
N			▓				S
F	▓	▓	▓	▓			T
P	▓	▓	▓				J

Honduran culture also is practical (S) and experiential (S).

Uruguay is ENFP:

Clear				Slight			Clear
I				▓	▓		E
N			▓				S
F			▓				T
P		▓	▓				J

Uruguayan culture also is receiving (I), intimate (I), realistic (S), traditional (S), critical (T), tough (T), and early starting (J).

Brazil is ENFP:

Clear			Slight			Clear
I				▓	▓	▓	E
N			▓				S
F		▓	▓				T
P	▓	▓	▓				J

Brazilian culture also is experiential (S), traditional (S) and questioning (T).

"Brazil is big and each part of the country received different migrants, so from the south for example the migration was made by German and Italians basically. From São Paulo till north is a big mix between Italian, Spanish, Africans, Dutch, French and Portuguese, but to simplify I believe we are more comfortable with Africans and personally I think we are very lucky about it."

"Whatever its origins, Brazilians are known for their informality, good nature, and charm (*simpatia*), as well as their desire not to be thought unpleasant or boorish (*chato*). They place high value on warmth, spontaneity, and lack of pomp and ceremony."—Brazil and its People, AFS Intercultura Brazil.

Ecuador is ENFP:

Clear			Slight			Clear
I				▓	▓	▓	E
N			▓				S
F			▓				T
P		▓	▓				J

Ecuadorian culture also is concrete (S), experiential (S), reasonable (T), questioning (T), and early starting (J).

Venezuela is ENFP:

Clear				Slight				Clear
I				▓	▓	▓		E
N			▓					S
F		▓						T
P	▓	▓	▓					J

Venezuelan culture also is traditional (S) and critical (T).

"As in most other countries with a relatively large territory and a multicultural base it all depends on the area of the country we are talking about. However, we tend to have most similarities with other Hispanic Caribbean countries (Colombia, Dominican Republic, Panama, Nicaragua, Cuba, Honduras, the Gulf and Caribbean coast of Mexico)."

MIDDLE EAST

Sudan is ENFP:

Clear				Slight				Clear
I				▓	▓	▓		E
N			▓					S
F		▓						T
P		▓						J

Sudanese culture also is quiet (I) and traditional (S).

Sudan is the tenth largest country in the world (by land area). Sudan is one of the most ethnically and linguistically diverse countries in the world. Sudanese culture melds the behaviors, practices, and beliefs of about 600 tribes, communicating in 142 different languages—it is microcosm of Africa.

Sudan is split between ENFP and ESFP with only a slight preference for either intuition or sensing. Sudanese clearly prefer extraversion and have many personal contacts. A Sudanese professor of anthropology reported Sudan as ENFP and commented, "When you take the bus, usually you end-up introducing yourself to the person sitting beside you, and most of the time, based on the response a conversation will be initiated, different topics. Based on mutual interest you can end-up having his/her phone number, and 10% I will say you end-up calling/meeting this person and develop a relationship at the family level."

"Mostly educated people and those who grow-up in major cities are more expressive and open to others. Village people usually hold back their engagement until they get to know you better, then they will become more involved at more openness in dealing with you without that civilization's protocols."

ENFPs are focused on relationships, community and a collective purpose. "People of Sudan are community oriented society; they act as groups at all concepts of life. For example, in big cities there are many tribe based organizations that brings people from the same region to work together (clubs, sport teams, societies in universities & major departments, etc). These groups work for their own well-being where they reside, and towards their regions, where they came from. On the other hand the same people will be found involved in many other groups in their wider community working towards the well-being of communities where they live (women unions, neighbourhood committees, youth groups, etc.)"

Extraverts are active, initiate contact and build bridges between people. "Sudanese people are known among Africans & Arabs as the most involved nation in politics, everyone is born and grows-up in a house where their father, brothers, and lately even mother & sisters are involved in political parties, unions or humanitarian organizations. This culture has made us very interactive communities, always seeking supporters or being targeted for votes."

Although clearly extraverts, the Sudanese do have an occasional introverted side. "Mainly our culture supports the quiet style in regards to the spotlights, they are overly humble, burying their talent with a negative quality (e.g. in western countries, most of us fail in job search because it's not our culture to speak highly about yourself or market your skills & qualifications). Sudanese are very active, energetic and very involved when it comes to sports and politics."

Sudanese reported a slight preference for intuition but economic need has brought out their sensing side. "Because of the economical stability for a long time, most people stepped back and lost enthusiasm to carry-on an active financial life until that stability was lost recently. Due to the financial pressure people have become more concrete in their life driven by economic & social facts."

Saudi Arabia is ENFP:

Clear				Slight				Clear
I				▓				E
N			▓					S
F			▓					T
P		▓						J

Saudi Arabian culture is contained (I), quiet (I), practical (S), logical (T), reasonable (T), and methodical (J).

Saudi Arabia's 2005 population is estimated to be about 26.5 million including about 5.5 million resident foreigners. Until the 1960s, most of the population was nomadic or seminomadic; due to rapid economic and urban growth, more than 95% of the population now is settled. Saudi Arabia is known as the birthplace of Islam, which in the century following Muhammad's death in 632, spread west up to Spain and east up to India. Ethnic groups are Arab (90%) and other (10%). The percentage of Muslim citizens is 100%. Sunni represent approximately 89% while Shiites represent approximately 11% of the population. Most Shiites live in the Eastern Province and are concentrated in some cities and villages such as Qatif and Najran.

Two university students reported Saudi culture as INTP and ISFJ and two responses from embassies both reported ENFP. I interviewed one student from the capital city of Riyadh. He refused to give me his name because he was afraid of reprisal by the Saudi Arabian royalty, and thought probably the other Saudi Arabian students wouldn't be willing to talk for the same reason. He said, "In Saudi Arabia there is a saying that the government knows more about you than you know about yourself."

Saudi's are contained and private. "People keep their ideas and opinions to themselves. Secrets are everything. In Saudi Arabia people don't joke about and shouldn't talk about personal matters. Islam is too strict (division between boys and girls, men and women, etc). You can't shake a woman's hand or touch them. If someone were sitting with his sister and you shook both their hands, the brother would try to kill you. Even on television you can see people being tortured and killed."

Saudis seem divided on their feeling and thinking preference. "Saudis make all their decisions with their head and no heart or feeling, they are completely different from any other middle eastern country (e.g. Syria, Lebanon, etc)." However, another Saudi said, "Saudi people are empathic, personal and seek understanding if it is a group they know. The personality of the country and the ways of living all come from religion. If a friend or someone needs money we will help them—it is part of the religion. This also is is why there are no homeless in Saudi Arabia."

Some of the Saudi laws can seem very tough-minded and impersonal. "If you are under 21 you can't travel out of the country alone—you must be with family and friends or get special permission. Single men aren't allowed to go into the shopping malls and movie theatres. Single men are hard pressed for things to do. The women aren't allowed to drive so the men end up driving them to the malls that men aren't allowed in." Small enterprises like taxis that specialize in transporting women are growing because women aren't allowed to drive. There is a need for businesses not centered on oil because they recognize the oil supply will eventually run out.

Saudis seem to have an intuitive bent towards education. "Everyone learns English after elementary but I learned from kindergarten. American university classes are more useful than Saudi universities." Sounds like Saudi universities might focus more on the theoretical (intuitive) whereas Americans teach more applied knowledge. "I studied at a Saudi university and it was very hard but I took two classes at an American private university without studying and aced them."

Saudi public funding of education is similar to some feeling European countries. "Saudi universities are free for Saudis and if you study something like science they even give you additional money to study. Before President Bush, the Saudis owed a lot of money to the US. Now they have an excess budget of 190 billion. With part of this money, they made a deal with the US to fund 50,000 scholarships for Saudis to study in the USA. This was part of a plan with the US to get Saudi students to come to the US to study again because it had dropped off after 9/11 and the restrictions put on by the US government on student visas."

12

ENTP—Extraverted Intuition plus Introverted Thinking

ENTPs use extraverted intuition and have a secondary preference for introverted thinking. We all use extraverted intuition when we explore new possibilities and form new ideas from the world around us. However, the ENTP uses it more and is likely to be better at it than other types. Extraverted intuition is what ENTPs use in the outer world and for interactions with others. ENTPs second preference is for introverted thinking. Introverted thinking types use inner principles and categories as guides to analyze and define the world. ENTPs use introverted thinking in their inner, private world so it's difficult to observe in their actions or words.

It doesn't matter how strongly you prefer extraverted intuition if your experience doesn't reflect what you are trying to gain insight into there will be little mature, cutting edge or inspiring responses from extraverted intuition. An extraverted intuitive with thinking may be good at seeing the possibilities for computers technology and the possibilities for starting and running a business, but extraverted intuition is only as good as the information you feed it. It is just like the muse: what you put in is what you get out. Feed quality information to person with a secondary preference for extraverted intuition (INFP or INTP) and you will get better results and ideas than from an ENTP or ENFP who has relatively little information or experience.

EUROPE

Lithuania is ENTP:

Clear				Slight			Clear
I				■	■		E
N			■				S
F				■	■		T
P			■				J

Lithuanian culture also is contained (I), experiential (S), traditional (S), tender (F), early starting (J) and scheduled (J). (The end of Chapter 2 has a decription of each facet.)

Serbia is ENTP:

Clear				Slight			Clear
I				■	■	■	E
N			■				S
F				■			T
P	■	■	■				J

Serbian culture also is practical (S), experiential (S), empathic (F), and compassionate (F).

Serbs reported themselves as clear extraverts, but were split down the middle between intuition and sensing. "We are traditional and customary, but also different and unusual at the same time. Belgrade was never a dull and grey city like other eastern capitals, and there were a lot of very original people there before the tragic split of Yugoslavia. When it came to problem solving, unconventionality was like a 'middle name' for people in Serbia—sometimes an unusual solution came out of sheer necessity or a lack of a technological resource."

Serbs as extraverted intuitive people can spontaneously come up with possible solutions to problems as they arise. "Our theatre was center point for a large worldwide known theatrical festival. Many times there was a need for improvising. Most of the festival was developed in non-theatrical spaces. We had to provide all the technical needs in a place where there were no renting companies, or special skills of company members. Things were solved thru invention, improvisation, friend's help, and everything that does not include money (as opposed to the normal way of doing things in west: you pay someone and he fixes it for you)."

Serbs are clearly perceiving types. Serbia is not an "organized, planned and strictly 'by the book society'. Laws are made to be broken, aren't they? Easy-going, in a calm waters, no fuss…it also is a part of Serbian national being."

MIDDLE EAST

Afghanistan is ENTP:

Clear				Slight			Clear
I				▓	▓		E
N	▓	▓					S
F			▓				T
P	▓	▓	▓				J

Afghani culture also is contained (I), traditional (S), empathic (F), and compassionate (F).

"On the whole, you will note that there is an interesting dichotomy among Afghans. They can be simultaneously reserved and sociable. It's not necessarily that they are hypocritical in nature, but I do think that there are interesting contradictions in how certain aspects of life are theorized and how they are practiced. This dichotomy is particularly noticeable in Afghan literature and music—where Afghans preach about modesty, chastity and virtue. Afghan stories/poems/music often present a reality that is intertwined in passion, longing, and forbidden love."

13

INFJ—Introverted Intuition plus Extraverted Feeling

The next two chapters are about the introverted intuition mental process. INFJs and INTJs prefer to use introverted intuition the majority of the time. Their second choice, in the case of the INFJ would be extraverted feeling, and for the INTJ extraverted thinking.

INFJs use introverted intuition and have a secondary preference for extraverted feeling. We all use introverted intuition because everyone has occasional flashes of insight or visions into what the future will hold. However, the INFJ uses it more and is likely to be better at it than other types. Introverted intuition is what INFJs use in their inner, private world so it's difficult to observe in their actions or words. INFJs second preference is for extraverted feeling. Extraverted feeling types take care others and strive for harmony in relationships. INFJs use extraverted feeling in the outer world and for interactions with others.

One Hungarian reported INFJ (and one INTJ) but they weren't the majority. Also, there was one INFJ response from Austria, which shares a border with Hungary. Maybe there is an INFJ subculture in or near one of these countries. A man from Bali also reported Indonesia as INFJ. Also, someone from Sweden reported INFJ—but Sweden is clearly sensing and ISFJ.

14

INTJ—Introverted Intuition plus Extraverted Thinking

INTJs use introverted intuition and have a secondary preference for extraverted thinking. We all use introverted intuition because everyone has occasional flashes of insight or visions into what the future will hold. However, the INTJ uses it more and is likely to be better at it than other types. Introverted intuition is what INTJs use in their inner, private world so it's difficult to observe in their actions or words. INTJs second preference is for extraverted thinking. Extraverted thinking types plan and logically organize projects and activities to achieve a goal. INTJs use extraverted thinking in the outer world and for interactions with others.

According to Myers, about one third of the American population is introverted and also about one third is intuitive (other sources state even lower percentages for both). Thinking and feeling types are evenly split but there are slightly more male thinking types and women are slightly more feeling types. Judging types outnumber perceiving types by about ten percent.

This also is is true for cultures: introverted and intuitive country types are the least common. There are two INFP countries but INFJ, INTJ and even INTP had no verified countries. For example, I received one response from France for INTJ and one for Hungary but these didn't agree with other people.

15

ESFP—Extraverted Sensing plus Introverted Feeling

The next two chapters are about the extraverted sensing mental process. ESFPs and ESTPs prefer to use extraverted sensing the majority of the time. Their second choice, in the case of the ESFP would be introverted feeling, and for the ESTP introverted thinking.

ESFPs use extraverted sensing and have a secondary preference for introverted feeling. We all use extraverted sensing when we engage all five senses, spontaneously interact with the world and live fully in the moment. However, the ESFP uses it more and is likely to be better at it than other types. Extraverted sensing is what ESFPs use in the outer world and for interactions with others. ESFPs second preference is for introverted feeling. Introverted feeling types use their inner value system to guide their actions and decisions. ESFPs use introverted feeling in their inner, private world so it's difficult to observe in their actions or words.

For ESFPs, social standing and social payoff can be a big motivator. They will maintain appearances with whomever or whatever group they are in. They are good at picking up cues in a social situation and reacting. They sometimes can't see the impact their actions and reaction have on others and as a result may suffer or succeed accordingly. The sensing type is tied to the here and now reality, and doesn't apply judgment to it. He or she just accepts it fully as it

is. In the extreme, other types might see this lack of judgment as a lack of ethics or understanding of right or wrong.

More than other country types, many ESFP countries have practices of animism, mysticism, shamanism, black magic, witch doctors, etc. For example, animism throughout the Pacific Islands, shamanism in Tibet and Korea, Mexicans love of mysticism, and Indonesian have black magic. Also, is it possible the ESFP Hawaiian conflict resolution process called *Ho'oponopono* could be used as tool for understanding, conflict resolution and healing between western countries and ESFP Muslim/Arabic societies?

Out of 115 countries, 37 countries (including the Pacific Islands) are ESFP. Fourteen of these ESFP countries (including Hawaii) are islands with populations all together totaling only about 13 million people. If you consider the billion populations of ENFP India or ISFP China the actual number of ESFP countries becomes less relevant.

CENTRAL AMERICA

Mexico is ESFP:

Clear				Slight			Clear
I				░	░	░	E
N				░			S
F	░	░	░				T
P	░	░	░				J

Mexican culture also is abstract (N) and imaginative (N). (The end of Chapter 2 has a decription of each facet.)

The Mexicans reported themselves uniformly and clearly as EFP. They have only a slight preference for sensing which isn't surprising because several Spanish speaking cultures in Latin American, South American, and Spain report themselves as either ENFP or ESFP.

Examples of the perceiving Mexicans are "the apparent chaos of all the Mexican way or organizing. In 1985 when we were organizing the first Mexican party of our civil society in the Netherlands we started looking up for a place, means organization participants and the invited people. The last day magically everything was ready and was one of the most spontaneous and even not perfectly organized the people were personally interested in the good development of this event."

They are casual and easily diverted. "Another event was at the primary school for mixed Mexican-Netherlands where I and my colleague from the Cultural Union met the last day in April 2005. We agreed to form a foundation and we are still waiting to have its first activity. So as you can seen creativity and spontaneity are in our character as Mexicans."

Guatemala is ESFP:

Clear				Slight			Clear	
I					▓	▓	▓	E
N					▓			S
F		▓	▓	▓				T
P	▓	▓	▓					J

Guatemalan culture also is abstract (N) and imaginative (N).

Guatemala is exactly the same as Mexico! Which isn't surprising since they border each other.

El Salvador is ESFP:

Clear				Slight			Clear	
I					▓	▓	▓	E
N					▓			S
F	▓	▓	▓					T
P	▓	▓	▓					J

Salvadoran culture also is original (N), logical (T), reasonable (T), and scheduled (J).

CARIBBEAN

Bahamas is ESFP:

Clear				Slight			Clear	
I					▓	▓		E
N					▓			S
F			▓	▓				T
P			▓	▓				J

Bahamian culture also is original (N) and early starting (J).

"I feel very strongly that having grown up in the Bahamas has given me security and friendliness in any social situation and a warmth and accessibility to laughter perhaps hindered in other cultures. Behind any Bahamian upbringing is the ever present Colonial pragmatism which may seek to suppress the individual and deny creativity but today's Bahamian learns to work from it and accept it as a strong cement foundation that can survive any hurricane and together with the deep Christian traditions can be seen as a secure background in which to reach out to the global environment."

Jamaica is ESFP:

Clear				Slight			Clear
I				▓	▓	▓	E
N				▓	▓		S
F		▓	▓				T
P	▓	▓					J

Jamaican culture also is imaginative (N), questioning (T), planful (J), and scheduled (J).

I received two responses from Jamaica: ESTJ and ESFP. I am leaning towards ESFP, because all the island countries report ESFP; also the surrounding countries, i.e. Bahamas and Central America, are ESFP.

Jamaicans are feeling types but are also questioning and tough. "Buying new products or trying new things some Jamaicans may want to know the history about this new product, place or food item so that their money is not wasted. Therefore, they would ask others or do some research. I think that Jamaicans are tough and firm about almost everything because we are not accustomed to showing our emotions as intensely as others; for instance, some Jamaican mothers try to inculcate a sense of independence in their children by allowing them to carry their school bags or allowing them to get up on their own after a slight fall."

Dominican Republic is ESFP:

Clear				Slight			Clear	
I					▓	▓	▓	E
N					▓			S
F		▓	▓					T
P	▓	▓	▓					J

Dominican culture also is imaginative (N) and conceptual (N).

SOUTH AMERICA

Chile is ESFP:

Clear				Slight			Clear	
I					▓	▓		E
N					▓			S
F			▓					T
P	▓	▓	▓					J

Chilean culture also is imaginative (N) and logical (T).

One Chilean reported INTP and another ESFP. I went with ESFP because Peru and Colombia are the same. On the other hand, Chile's neighbor Argentina is ESTP and one Argentinian also reported INTP. Maybe Chile is INTP or there is a region, somewhere in Argentina or Chile, that is INTP.

Like all of South America, Chile is clearly a perceiving type. "I can think of two examples that can demonstrate the easy going type of the Chilean people, one of this is the famous: 'maniana' (mañana) which means tomorrow, nothing is done immediately or on the spot everything is left to be done tomorrow, and doesn't mean the day after because the day after again will be tomorrow, and so on forever until the last minute."

"There is a joke going on about Chileans and goes like this. Several countries were given an assignment to prepare a report, every country presented the assignment in excellent conditions one better than the other, when the time came for the Chilean to present his report he exclaimed: 'Don't tell me it was for today'."

Peru is ESFP:

Clear				Slight			Clear
I				▓	▓	▓	E
N				▓	▓		S
F	▓	▓	▓				T
P		▓	▓				J

Peruvian culture also is abstract (N) and imaginative (N).

The majority of people reported Peru as ESFP although I did get a couple of ESFJs. This is a classic ESFP: "I think Peruvian people, preserving their own characteristics, is like the rest of Latin-Americans: enjoy life, very open-mind and relaxed. They are happy people in general, very alive, find the opportunity to celebrate. Girls like to show their beauty. Beauty is very important in this country. They always celebrate any little thing. They live in the present as they don't know if they will have money to eat/survive tomorrow."

They clearly prefer extraversion. "When you sit in the bus it is not strange that people try to start a conversation and be your friend. When you come as a tourist everybody try to be your friend. People are sociable and talk to you in the streets."

First and foremost Peruvians are extraverted sensors. "It easier for them to talk about concrete things that they can see or feel with the senses. They learn from their work in general, in other words from their experience." As extraverted sensors they are practical and traditional. "They are more interested to work and earn money, as most of them live in miserable conditions. They are very religious and follow it strongly." Yet they also have an intuitive side and seek novelty. "They like imported and new things from other countries, especially from the USA and Europe."

Peruvians have a secondary preference for introverted feeling. "Neighbors listen to you if you have a problem. Friends are loyal to you and remember you forever. They try to help you always even though they don't have money." They are accommodating to their detriment. "For example, Indians accept to be dominated of white people and they work for them as servants." They also have a critical side. "They are skeptical as there is so much corruption that they don't believe in anybody."

Peruvians are perceiving types. "Without pressure nothing happens. Things are done in the last minute. They need someone to control them. As the political situation is so instable they get use to be very flexible and to be able to adapt to new things, also as a survival method. They have to do anything to find everyday's bread. There are already many cultures and variety of races, so people are used to variety."

Colombia is ESFP:

Clear				Slight			Clear
I				▓	▓	▓	E
N				▓	▓		S
F		▓	▓				T
P	▓	▓	▓				J

Colombian culture also is questioning (T).

Guyana is ESFP:

Clear				Slight			Clear
I				▓	▓	▓	E
N				▓			S
F	▓	▓	▓				T
P	▓	▓	▓				J

Guyanese culture also is abstract (N) and imaginative (N).

EUROPE

Portugal is ESFP:

Clear				Slight			Clear
I				▓	▓	▓	E
N				▓			S
F			▓				T
P	▓	▓	▓				J

Portuguese culture also is quiet (I), abstract (N), and critical (T).

As with many European countries, in Portugal, there had been a degree of admixture from other European nations, past and present, namely French, German, English, Scottish, Irish, Dutch and Flemish, Italian and Spanish. People from the former colonies (namely India, Africa and Brazil) have, in the last two to three decades, migrated to Portugal. More recently, a great number of Slavs, especially Ukrainians (now the biggest ethnic minority), are also migrating to Portugal. (*Wikipedia*)

There was a bit of a mix on what Portuguese thought, some said ENTP, ESTP, or ENFP but the majority was ESFP. "Portuguese are similar to or get along with Brazil, Spain, Italy, Angola, Mozambique." The first three countries are ENFP. The Portuguese have only a slight preference for sensing and feeling but clearly prefer extraversion and perceiving. "Think for instance in 2004—football, and in 1998—the World Exhibition—days before looked everything as it would be chaos, but it turned out to be great success."

One Dutch-speaking Belgian commented, "This example is not only Portuguese I think. This has been said about many cultures. I think of the Greek when they had their Olympics in 2004 or the Italians last winter." That is because these are all perceiving type countries including the Dutch-speaking Belgians!

Romania is ESFP:

Clear				Slight			Clear
I				▓	▓	▓	E
N				▓			S
F			▓				T
P	▓	▓	▓				J

Romanian culture also is abstract (N), imaginative (N), and reasonable (T).

"Congratulations for the daring endeavor of reading the Romanian mind! As Romanians we often feel like born in a melting pot of Western traditions and Oriental cultures. I encourage you to daringly explore the results of that magic alchemy." The Romanians are a difficult one to puzzle out. I received several response from Romanians: 5 ESFP, 3 ENTP, 1 ESTP, and 1 ENFP.

The ethnic groups in Romania are: Romanian (89.5%), Hungarian (6.6%), Roma (2.5%), German (0.3%,) and Ukrainian (0.3%). One person said, "I don't think Romania has major regional differences or subcultures." The Hungarian responses were very different from Romanians so I don't think their subculture in Romania was the reason for the variety of responses. Romanians are like the Portuguese and have only a slight preference for sensing and feeling but are clearly extraversion and perceiving.

An example of the perceiving Romanians being pressure prompted: "I would say the events in December 1989 and the way how whole Romanian society reacted at that time could be an example. 'Polenta exploded!' After so many years of quiet sufferance, the nation stood up for freedom and democracy."

The Romanian as extraverted sensing types engage all their senses and live fully in the moment. "Here's a personal example I thought it might be useful for being enthusiastic and experiential: The sun eclipse in 1999 (August) everybody gathered in the mountains by the town of Rimnicu Vilcea, the place of greatest eclipse duration. We were very enthusiastic about it, as it happens very rarely. We were all keen to see everything and then discussed about it. It was a major event at that time, even the press/tv presented it in detail."

Lastly, Romanians can also be conceptual (intuition). "As knowledge of the spiritual and intellectual profile of a people is key element in building bridges of dialogue, I do appreciate your initiative."

Macedonia is ESFP:

Clear				Slight			Clear
I				▓	▓	▓	E
N				▓			S
F			▓				T
P		▓	▓				J

Macedonian culture also is abstract (N), conceptual (N), questioning (T) critical (T), and systematic (J).

Greece is ESFP:

Clear				Slight			Clear
I				▓	▓	▓	E
N				▓	▓		S
F			▓				T
P	▓	▓	▓				J

Greek culture also is abstract (N), critical (T), and tough (T).

I talked with a big, outgoing, Greek guy with dark, curly hair. He said, "Greeks don't follow rules—they tend to break them. They are willing to accept everybody. They are passionate—especially about sports. They are unorganized and live in the moment and smoke a lot. They are into politics and not afraid to express themselves which can lead to conflict."

This book includes 32 out of a total 48 countries in Europe, and Greece, Malta and Portugal are the only ESFP countries. If we include ESTP Albania there are only four extraverted sensing cultures in Europe. The absence of extroverted sensing (ESFP and ESTP) countries in Europe may explain their difficulty with extroverted sensing cultures like the ESP Muslims. The US may have less of a problem because the US has an enormous Mexican population and shares its entire southern border with ESFP Mexico.

Malta is ESFP:

Clear				Slight			Clear
I				▓	▓	▓	E
N				▓			S
F		▓	▓				T
P	▓	▓	▓				J

Maltese culture also is abstract (N).

Malta is a small island off the coast of Italy. Here is an example of the Maltese people being compassionate (feeling): "Despite the fact that Maltese families have an average income when compared to other European countries, people tend to be very generous when catastrophes occur in other parts of the world." The Maltese are also extraverted. "The Maltese people are very expressive and initiating, while waiting at a bus stop or sitting in a bus, people start chatting as if they have known each other for years."

MIDDLE EAST

Turkey is ESFP:

Clear				Slight			Clear
I				▓	▓	▓	E
N				▓			S
F	▓	▓	▓				T
P	▓	▓	▓				J

Turkish culture also is questioning (T).

Turks are clearly extraverts. "There is one example for being expressive, even for initiating and active. It is very typical with Turkish people. For example, it happens very often that a person sits next to you when waiting at a bus stop and starts talking about his/her life and problems. Such dialogues are very common: 'I am now coming from hospital. I have problem with .... and the doctor said ......' and the other person replies, 'Oh, sorry to hear that. My uncle had the same problem. He got treatment at X Hospital and there the doctor did .....', and the dialogue goes on. Or another one saying, 'I have a daughter-in-law who I never wish anyone to have. The other day she said .....' The other person replies 'My daughter-in-law does not respect anyone either. She tells her husband, my son, to.....' and it goes on."

As feeling types they tend to get personal with others. "People don't mind talking about daily problems to a total stranger or asking about all personal issues such as family and kids. It is very common to continue socializing after such a dialogue and become friends. I, myself, have a close friend from a flight to Ankara 3 years ago, for example. We became friends when we started to talk about Stockholm and Ankara and of course someone she really liked and left behind in Stockholm. Not to mention my mother who makes friends daily in the street." Turkish people are so good at talking out their problems with others that "therapists in the country don't really get many patients except the specific cases in big cities."

Turks are perceiving types. "An example of being emergent can be the long long long lines the last day of a certain deadline. People usually wait for very long hours in lines (5-8 hours) on the last day of some application, rather than dealing with it 1 month earlier when there was no one, for example."

Cyprus is ESFP:

Clear				Slight				Clear
I				▓	▓	▓		E
N				▓				S
F		▓	▓					T
P	▓	▓	▓					J

Cypriot culture also is abstract (N) and theoretical (N).

Cyprus is a small island off the coast of Turkey. They are ESFP just like all the other islands countries in the Pacific Ocean, Indian Ocean, Caribbean Sea, Mediterranean Sea, etc.

Yemen is ESFP:

Clear				Slight			Clear
I				■	■	■	E
N				■	■	■	S
F		■	■				T
P			■				J

Yemeni culture also is logical (T), early starting (J) and scheduled (J).

AFRICA

Tanzania is ESFP:

Clear				Slight			Clear
I				■	■	■	E
N				■	■		S
F		■	■				T
P		■	■				J

Tanzanian culture also is imaginative (N) and reasonable (T).

This represents responses from across the country: the cities of Kilimanjaro, Arusha (both on the northern border with Kenya) and the capital of Dar-es Salaam.

Malawi is ESFP:

Clear				Slight			Clear
I				■			E
N				■	■		S
F			■				T
P			■				J

Malawian culture also is receiving (I), intimate (I), abstract (N), logical (T), reasonable (T), early starting (J) and scheduled (J).

Gambia is ESFP:

Clear				Slight				Clear
I				▓	▓			E
N				▓	▓			S
F			▓					T
P			▓					J

Gambian culture also is contained (I), imaginative (N), logical (T), reasonable (T), early starting (J), and methodical (J).

Muslims constitute more than 90% of the population.

Madagascar is ESFP:

Clear				Slight				Clear
I				▓	▓			E
N				▓				S
F	▓	▓	▓					T
P	▓	▓	▓					J

Malagasy culture also is contained (I), conceptual (N), and original (N).

Mauritius is ESFP:

Clear				Slight				Clear
I				▓	▓	▓		E
N				▓	▓	▓		S
F		▓	▓					T
P		▓	▓					J

Mauritian culture also is logical (T) and early starting (J).

South Africa is ESFP:

Clear				Slight			Clear
I				██	██	██	E
N				██			S
F	██	██	██				T
P	██	██	██				J

South African culture also is imaginative (N) and original (N).

South Africa is a nation of more than 47 million people of diverse origins, cultures, languages, and beliefs. The racial groups are Black African (79.4%), White (9.3%), Colored (mixed race) (8.8%), and Indian or Asian (2.5%).

ASIA

Philippines is ESFP:

Clear				Slight			Clear
I				██	██		E
N				██	██	██	S
F	██	██	██				T
P			██				J

Philippine culture also is receiving (I), imaginative (N), and early starting (J) and methodical (J).

I talked with several Filipino UH students. There are three regional groups of people in the Philippines: Tagalogs, Visayans, and Ilocanos. One Filipino lady (who was Tagalog) reported ESTJ, however the rest reported ESFP for the Philippines.

One older lady thought, "The Philippines was a Spanish colony for a hundred years. Filipinos are similar to Central Americans. Also, Filipino students hang out with more Central Americans than Asians." Central Americans reported the same type as the Filipinos.

She said "Ilocanos are in the North and value education, a big house, etc." I am from the central zone and clothes, earrings (appearances) are more important." Tagalogs are in the south. Farther down is the Visayan and the farthest south is Mindanao, which are mostly Muslims.

A Tagalog male said, "Filipinos get along great with Indonesians—maybe because of some are Christian and Catholics. Also, Filipinos Muslims adhere to the Muslim code more. They will look more for 'halal' Muslim food compared to Indonesian and Malaysian Muslims."

"Filipinos are like Americans and love Americans. Filipinos are probably similar to Latin Americans because they were both colonies of Spain. There are so many Ilocanos in the US and Hawaii because Marcos made a deal with the US immigration and his people (the Ilocanos) moved to the US more than any other Filipino group. Also, the Ilocanos are more explorers and they come from an area of the mountains where living is a hardship. The Tagalogs come from the plains where it is easier living and they are homebodies. The Ilocanos are more hard working, stingy, adventurous and have the confidence to go live in other areas." A Visayan girl said, "Among the Visayans there is a subgroup called the Ilonggo that are more risk takers and outgoing." He said, "Both the Tagalogs and Visayans are also outgoing."

A Visayan girl from Manila said, "One interesting trait about Filipinos is we are all afraid of rain because we might catch a cold. One Filipino anthropologist Micheal Tan (Chinese) who writes for the Filipino Daily newspaper, said the cold virus is actually in the areas they go for cover from the rain." Her Tagalog male friend mentioned, "Also, National Geographic had a survey of Asian people and Filipinos were famous for their fear of heights."

Tibet is ESFP:

Clear				Slight			Clear
I				▓	▓		E
N				▓	▓		S
F		▓	▓				T
P			▓				J

Tibetan culture also is quiet (I), abstract (N), logical (T), early starting (J) and scheduled (J).

I interviewed a Tibetan UH student. According to her, they relate bad news to Buddhist ideas and filter everything through their Buddhist understanding. Sensing types relate perceptions to previous understanding and experience. "For example, when friend dies you are sad, it's karma, it's the time for him and inevitable, nothing is wrong, pray for him to get a new life and reincarnate as a human, not as an animal. Animals can't understand Buddhist teaching so it takes many lifetimes to reincarnate again as a human."

Tibetans as sensing types follow traditional Buddhist ways. "Tibetans are realistic (in a Buddhist way) because they believe your day to day life is the effect of your previous lives (reincarnation). My sister's daughter is the reincarnate of her grandmother. She talked about my grandmother even though she had never met the grand-mother because she died before her birth."

Tibetans are sensing but they also have a preference for intuition's abstract facet. "Tibetan Buddhism is from India and is mixed with Tibetan shamanism but meanings are derived from Buddhism. We relate everything to Buddhist symbols."

"Quiet and compassion (introversion and feeling facets) are from Buddhism." The core of Buddhism is compassion and the source of Tibetans feeling preference. They are feeling types but also have a thinking preference for objective analysis, discussion and being tough-minded. "Tibetans are logical and they try to understand everything through Buddhist logic. Tibetans are accommodating but discussion is part of Buddhist teaching."

"There is a story of how Buddhism came to Tibet. An Indian Buddhist Lama and a Chinese Buddhist Lama came to Tibet. The Tibetan people asked the two to debate and they would follow the winner of the debate. The debate lasted several days and they chose Indian Buddhism as the winner. Tibetan Buddhism follows Indian Buddhism and not Chinese—there is no Chinese Buddhism in Tibet."

Tibetans are tender but tough-minded. "When talking to other people of other religions they can be tough-minded. This doesn't mean they aren't open. Just that they see everything according to Buddhism and if another religion doesn't fit the Buddhist frame-work they resist it in their mind." Sensing types have a hard time coping with things outside of their experience and frame of reference.

Tibetans extraverts and "very social but don't introduce each other and don't know each other's names. They also have a fixed social circle. Tibetans are open to try to understand other cultures, but understanding is found through where it fits in their Buddhist perspective. When the Christian missionaries arrived Tibetans felt discussion of the Christian religion was okay. They tried to understand Jesus but they couldn't until they put it into a Buddhist perspective." Sensing types can have a difficulties with abstract ideas until they can relate it to their own experience and then it becomes understandable.

"Tibetans tried to find a position for Jesus in Buddhism. Then they realized that he is a Bodhisattva. Tibetans always think from a Buddhism perspective and now many think that Jesus is a Bodhisattva—there are many Bodhisattvas. Jesus was a Bodhisattva because he was good and also sacrificed himself for the sins of the people."

Bangladesh is ESFP:

Clear				Slight			Clear
I				■	■		E
N				■			S
F			■				T
P		■	■				J

Bangladeshi culture also is intimate (I), critical (T), and systematic (J).

Thailand is ESFP:

Clear				Slight			Clear
I				■	■		E
N				■			S
F	■	■	■				T
P	■	■	■				J

Thai culture also is imaginative (N).

"Thais are sociable and congenial that's why we are called the land of smile." Thais are the Mexicans of South East Asia with a clear feeling and perceiving preference, and slightly sensing with a preference for imagination (intuition). Thais are obviously extraverted sensing types with their sense of humor, love of *sanuk* (fun) and desire to enjoy life to the fullest.

Sri Lanka is ESFP:

Clear				Slight			Clear
I				■			E
N				■			S
F			■				T
P		■	■				J

Sri Lankan culture also is quiet (I), conceptual (N), theoretical (N), logical (T), and early starting (J).

One Sri Lankan UH student said, "Many values come from Buddhism in Sri Lanka like the compassionate and quiet facets." This is the same thing the Tibetan student said about Buddhism in Tibetan culture.

East Timor is ESFP:

Clear				Slight			Clear
I				▓	▓		E
N				▓	▓		S
F			▓				T
P		▓	▓				J

East Timorian culture also is critical (T).

The culture of East Timor reflects numerous cultural influences, including Portuguese, Roman Catholic, Malay, and the indigenous Austronesian and Melanesian. Portuguese and Melanesian cultures (Solomon Islands) are also ESFP. In East Timor (a former Portuguese colony) 95% of the people are Catholic whereas their neighbor Indonesia is 87% Muslim. One UH student said, "The war with Indonesia was because of political differences and not religious ones."

"All the Brazilians (ENFP) we talk with, we get along with it. It is a perfect match, for example, when we are talking and eating with Brazilians. We also get along with people from Mozambique and other Portuguese speaking countries." For sensing he pointed out that, "Guests dress right and don't involve themselves in family problems. The etiquette of the guests is from the European influence mainly Portugal."

He picked the tender and compassionate facets of the feeling preference and gave an example of East Timorans being sympathetic and tender-hearted: "There were militia from East Timor that actually fought against East Timor. When they came back home to East Timor they were accepted back into the community (of course if they confessed and showed regret)."

They also have a thinking side and can be critical. "If an East Timorian hates you they show it, the Indonesians don't. Also, in the western part of East Timor they discuss and think more than the east."

Indonesia is ESFP:

Clear				Slight			Clear
I				▓			E
N				▓			S
F			▓				T
P		▓	▓				J

Indonesian culture also is quiet (I), abstract (N), imaginative (N), tough (T), systematic (J) and planful (J).

Indonesia's population is 245 million and is the fourth largest in the world (after the USA). Indonesians are 87% Muslim and have several ethnic groups: Javanese (41.7%), Sundanese (15.4%), Malay (3.4%), Madurese (3.3%), Batak (3.0%), Minangkabau (2.7%), Betawi (2.5%), Buginese (2.5%), Bantenese (2.1%), Banjarese (1.7%), Balinese (1.5%), Sasak (1.3%), Makassarese (1.0%), Cirebon (0.9%), Chinese (0.9%), Others (16.1%).

One South Sulanesi man who is studying sociology said, "Java has the most population and may be the most representative of Indonesia. Bali also is a big population center. East Timor and Eastern Indonesian characters are similar: easygoing, active, and enthusiastic. Also, Indonesians are more passive in the rural areas."

Australia is ESFP:

Clear				Slight			Clear
I				▓	▓	▓	E
N				▓			S
F		▓	▓				T
P		▓	▓				J

Australian culture also is imaginative (N), original (N), questioning (T), and early starting (J).

Here are three responses I received from Australians:
2 ESFP (from Melbourne)
1 ENFP (from Canberra)

Australia-English culture is ESTJ:

Clear				Slight			Clear
I				▒	▒	▒	E
N				▒	▒		S
F				▒	▒		T
P				▒			J

Australian-English culture also is original (N) and casual (P). (This is similar to USA.)

Here are four additional responses I received from Australians:
2 ESTJ (from Perth and Sydney)
1 ISTJ (also from Canberra)
ESTx (location not mentioned)

Most of the estimated 20.6 million Australians are descended from nineteenth- and twentieth-century immigrants, the majority from Great Britain and Ireland. Ireland is ENFP and Great Britain is ESTJ. The surrounding countries of Oceania/Pacific Islands are ESFP including New Zealand so maybe the underlying or indigenous culture of Australia is ESFP.

"Australian people have in the past tended to adopt the British way of living in general sense but this mainly applies to the higher levels of this society, when it comes to the average 'block' (person) they tend to have a much lighter and easy going attitude towards life. Some of the usual slants are 'she'll be right mate' meaning 'do not worry too much about, it will be OK tomorrow'. A few more that apply are 'don't worry be happy' or 'no worries mate' or 'everything is Honky Dory' (no translation) meaning everything is bright and shiny."

The average 'block' person is ESFP, whereas the 'higher level society' with British ways is ESTJ. Therefore, Australian culture is both ESFP and ESTJ.

An ESFP example of perceiving: "I guess we could compare the Portuguese experience (of being pressure prompted in getting ready for the 2004 football and the 1998 World Exhibition) and with something similar that happened here just before the 2000 Olympics. On most similar cases the national pride overcomes the possible problems arising when your country is involved on such type of projects, we know for sure that we are being watched by the rest of the world."

An ESTJ example of being planful and scheduled: "Living in Greece at the moment helps me see the differences in Sydney culture a lot clearer. People living in Sydney always plan their social schedules ahead of time—even something as simple as making a phone call is usually planned and announced—for example, you might bump into a friend on the street and after a conversation you will say 'I'll call you next Wednesday so that we can arrange to catch up'. Spontaneity is rare—people are not likely to just drop by your house for a visit or call you at the last minute to ask you if you're interested in going out. On average, people know what they are doing at least a week in advance and don't like their schedules being disrupted. They also want to know exactly where they will meet, what time and how they will be getting there ahead of time. Any Australian person would find this kind of social planning normal—ask a Greek their opinion though and they'll think it's absurd!!!"

OCEANIA/PACIFIC ISLANDERS

Polynesia

Hawaiians are ESFP:

Clear				Slight			Clear
I				▓	▓	▓	E
N				▓	▓	▓	S
F		▓	▓				T
P		▓	▓				J

It is fair to say Hawaii is a country all of its own and deserves separate consideration from the mainland USA. Hawaii is one the most multi-ethnic communities in the world so the type of the

Hawaiians may not represent the local culture or may only be the 'shared' type between the many other ethnic cultures in Hawaii.

UH professor Ray Moody determined the Hawaiians to be ESTP through MBTI testing of 50 Hawaiian college students. According to Moody, the hyperactivity, unpredictability, playing to an audience and having fun of the Hawaiian children in the classroom typify an ESTP. "Equality is a central element in Hawaiian culture. Peers are absolutely equal. To try to appear better than someone else is inappropriate, wholly unacceptable behavior." In Hawaiian culture equality and solidarity are achieved through a process of individual and group rivalry as opposed to individual competition. Yet one must still be friendly, generous and humble. "Rivalry... action, spontaneity, a ready challenge to authority, toughness, all stirred together to create a way of being that is just plain fun—ESTP fun."

Based on responses from Hawaiians and other Pacific Islanders they are ESFP—an extraverted sensing and introverted feeling culture. Hawaiian culture has been destroyed and it is difficult to see without looking to their history—this is where we can see the ESFP

Hawaiian clearly. In their canoe building we can see the SP craftsman; and in their hula dance and *mele* (sing, chant) we can see the ESFP performer. Their traditions of talk story and luau parties are examples of their preference for extraverted sensing and extroversion.

"Hawaiian women gave freely of their sexual bounty (Pukui, *Nānā i ke kumu*—Look to the source). "ESFPs can appear fickle, even promiscuous, to other types, when in truth they are simply, and rather innocently, sharing with others from the bounty of life" (Keirsey, *Please Understand Me II*). Hawaiians have an Aloha spirit of being helpful (*kokua*), friendly, generous (*lokomaikai*), and humble (*ha'aha'a*), and as ESFPs can be generous even to their detriment.

Ho'oponopono is a classic example of the introverted feeling of the Hawaiians. It involves prayer, conflict resolution, being genuine, absolute truth and honesty, confessions, restitution, genuine forgiveness, and spiritual closure. Hawaiians value harmony (*lokahi*), love of family (*ohana*), love of the land, spirituality, concern for children's welfare and physical affection for children—all feeling traits.

Introverted feeling types are altruists and idealists. "Some say that the Great Mahele stands out in Hawaiian history as an extraordinary example of altruism, for the Hawaiian aristocracy peacefully relinquished many of their hereditary rights and privileges for the good of the people." (Diane Lee Rhodes, Overview of Hawaiian History)

Other examples of introverted feeling are the Hawaiians and other Pacific Islanders belief in dreams. "C.G. Jung believed this: that dreams will show where the unconscious is leading us and point to an end. Thus, Hawaiian belief in and work with dreams is more consonant with the philosophy of Jung than with that of Freud" (Young, *People and Cultures of Hawaii*).

One social worker involved with Hawaiians and Pacific Islanders (at a Hawaii school) said after the Bikini Atoll bomb testing the government felt bad and starting giving out a lot of government assistance (housing, welfare, etc,) in Hawaii and now they have learned to be dependant on government assistance. Both myself and HPU psychology professor Ostrowski, as INFPs, believe the Hawaiians haven't been given a chance to use their god given gifts (ESFP gifts) and that those gifts aren't rewarded in a way that they consider reward, like giving them more social standing. At Kamehameha schools, a new teaching system was developed for Hawaiian culture, but Hawaii has yet to develop a system of employment and reward that fits the Hawaiian culture.

It's obvious Hawaiian/Pacific island culture is perceiving. They work in very different ways from judging types like the Caucasians and Asians. In the Hawaiian *uku pau* system you get your share of work done and you're finished for the day—this clashes with judging types belief in a set schedule.

Subjectivity is a feeling trait, decisions are based on internal values as opposed to external facts. According to Patrick Ka'ano'i, in his book *The Need for Hawaii*, Hawaii is a subjective culture, "Like individuals, cultures are also primarily subjective or objective. The culture that primarily values technology or individualism is definitely objective, while a culture that values the family, nature, and the celebration of life is surely identified as subjective. Whether you are Hawaiian or not, if you primarily relate to life and people on a personal level, you are subjective and have a major conflict of interest in the present Western objective style of ethics." This is a classic thinker-feeler conflict.

Lastly, Ka'ano'i provides a solution for the Native Hawaiians that are living marginalized in their own land: "The secret of a subjective individual or culture within an objective one is simply to draw a circle bigger than the one that shuts you out. Don't be afraid of objective tools or systems, for it is the subjective self that empowers them, not the other way around. Government, money, and technology are not human, and don't make the mistake of thinking they are. Use them creatively, and you will command your life, family and culture." A case for individual feeling types and feeling ethnic groups marginalized in thinking cultures.

New Zealand is ESFP:

Clear				Slight			Clear
I				░	░	░	E
N				░			S
F		░	░				T
P		░	░				J

New Zealand culture also is imaginative (N), original (N), questioning (T), and early starting (J).

The New Zealander can be questioning and uses this in service to their feeling preference. "In terms of challenging and wanting discussion as well as harmony, I think there a few political examples of this. We still see these days that a majority of the country is behind the 1981 (I think it was '81) banning of nuclear powered ships into New Zealand waters. At the time this was certainly a challenge to the power of the United States yet New Zealand has never backed down. Our role as peacekeepers in the world highlights the desire for global harmony, we have forces in East Timor at the moment and I believe there are still NZ peacekeeping/rebuilding forces in Afghanistan despite the NZ government's opposition of the actual war. I think the desire for harmony and discussion can also be seen closer to home when we look at inter-racial interaction over the past few decades. There has been more outrage and demonstrations in previous years against certain government policy but there has also been much discussion throughout the country."

"In terms of extraversion all I can really say is that every foreigner I meet overseas who has been to New Zealand talks of the friendliness of the people, their willingness to engage with tourists and their willingness to help."

New Zealanders have a slight preference for sensing, so can also be intuitive. "In terms of imaginative/inventive, I believe that recently a New Zealand man has been travelling the length of the country in his car which he is now running on used Fish 'n Chip oil (I think it is to do with the ongoing escalation of petrol prices in NZ). NZ can be seen as unconventional. I believe we are the first government to have a trans-sexual MP (Member of Parliament). This also is displays the accepting, tolerant nature of New Zealand society. In past work places I've always found my bosses to be tolerant and they readily give praise."

"NZ'ers are very easy going and relaxed. I was once greeted at NZ international Airport with 'how are things going'! As well as being casual I think we are very flexible and are 'non-complainers' and get down to the job."

Cook Islands is ESFP:

Clear				Slight			Clear	
I					▓	▓	▓	E
N					▓	▓	▓	S
F	▓	▓	▓	▓				T
P		▓	▓					J

Cook Islander culture also is intimate (I) and methodical (J).

American Samoa is ESFP:

Clear				Slight			Clear	
I				▓	▓	▓		E
N				▓	▓			S
F		▓	▓					T
P		▓	▓					J

American Samoan culture also is abstract (N), critical (T), and tough (T).

"Samoans are generally sociable, congenial, and love to introduce people. You can witness this yourself if you'd like to visit a village in Samoa. Strangers are welcomed. Young and old alike would not hesitate to speak with you and ask you your name and where you are from and may end up asking you to join them for a meal to introduce you to the family."

Melanesia

Solomon Islands is ESFP:

Clear				Slight			Clear
I				▓	▓		E
N				▓	▓	▓	S
F			▓				T
P		▓	▓				J

Solomon Islander culture also is reflective (I), questioning (T), critical (T), and early starting (J).

The half a million people on the Solomon Islands are ethnically Melanesian (94.5%), Polynesian (3%) and Micronesian (1.2%). The ESFP type is "to an extent true for the good majority of Solomon Islanders. However, the newer generations who are educated and who work and live in towns and in the capital city, Honiara, do organise themselves, introduce themselves, are active and strategise and plan activities and appreciate early start on activities as compared to the about 80% of people who live in the rural communities. The 80% enjoy an easy, un-routine, unscheduled lifestyle. Solomon Islanders feel comfortable speaking to strangers at a distance of 3 meters (space). Normally, the older generation Solomon Islanders do not appreciate the shaking of hands as a gesture of greeting and welcome. You just smile to them and proceed to say hullo or good morning and ask for directions or ask questions. Husbands, especially of older generations, do not appreciate strangers shaking their wives' hands. Touching females is restricted by cultural taboo." (Alfred Manengelea Lovanitila, Assistant Secretary of Foreign Affairs Solomon Islands)

Fiji is ESFP:

Clear				Slight			Clear
I				▓	▓	▓	E
N				▓	▓		S
F		▓	▓				T
P	▓	▓	▓				J

Fijian culture also is imaginative (N) and conceptual (N).

Fiji is part of Melanesia (along with Solomon Islands). A single Fijian reported ENFP for the culture with a slight preference for intuition. Is Fiji is different from the rest of the Pacific Islands—that are all ESFP—including Melanesia? I'm guessing ESFP.

"Generally speaking, Fijians are warm, friendly and hospitable, a common characteristics of South Pacific islanders. Greeting even strangers with a warm smile and *bula* (hello) is a common practice."

Micronesia

Marshall Islands is ESFP:

Clear				Slight			Clear
I				▓			E
N				▓	▓	▓	S
F		▓	▓				T
P		▓	▓				J

Marshall Islander culture also is intimate (I), reflective (I), reasonable (T), and planful (J).

"Micronesians are more outgoing than the Hawaiians." The Americans average family size (in the home) is two, Hawaiian three and Samoan four. "Micronesians value extended family even more than the Hawaiians and Samoans."

16

ESTP—Extraverted Sensing plus Introverted Thinking

ESTPs use extraverted sensing and have a secondary preference for introverted thinking. We all use extraverted sensing when we engage all five senses, spontaneously interact with the world and live fully in the moment. However, the ESTP uses it more and is likely to be better at it than other types. Extraverted sensing is what ESTPs use in the outer world and for interactions with others. ESTPs second preference is for introverted thinking. Introverted thinking use inner principles and categories as guides to analyze and define the world. ESTPs use introverted thinking in their inner, private world so it's difficult to observe in their actions or words.

All of the ESTP countries except for Iceland had an out-of-preference for imaginative maybe this is because extroverted sensors are well known as story tellers and can be creative in their search for fun and excitement. Also, many ESTP countries are Muslim.

SOUTH AMERICA

Argentina is ESTP:

Clear				Slight			Clear
I				▓	▓	▓	E
N				▓			S
F				▓			T
P	▓	▓	▓				J

Argentinian culture also is abstract (N), imaginative (N), empathic (F), and compassionate (F). (The end of Chapter 2 has a decription of each facet.)

"I have to say, that to analyze my culture is not easy. Our country is big (actually I think is the eighth biggest); therefore we have different cultures according with the region. But in general we have common behaviors with other Latin countries: friendly people, open and very informal. But among Latin American countries we are considered the coldest and most European one." This is probably because they are the only thinking type country in Latin America.

Argentines reported themselves consistently as ETP—the majority said ESTP but several also said ENTP. I speculate a regional difference for sensing and intuition. One response was from Ushuaia, the capital of Argentina's province of Tierra del Fuego, considered the world's southernmost city. Maybe intuitive types are in the southern part of Argentina. This is near Antarctica (south pole) just like the Eskimos (Greenland) are intuitive and in the Artic circle (north pole).

As sensing types (although only slightly) they are literal-minded. "Language is used in a very direct and literal way. In English sometimes people say 'that is not very nice' to mean that something is 'bad' ...if we mean 'bad' we say 'bad'." Argentines are extraverted sensors yet several people also reported intuition: "People don't have many resources so they need to be imaginative. The economic situation makes people resourceful to try and meet ends. For example, people who can't find a permanent job come up with things to sell in the street or things to do on a temporary basis to earn money."

"There's a big contrast between the way we behave and what we are taught. Our country has been greatly influenced by the Catholic Church, but we are more relaxed than the Saxons with their Victorian education. I know this because my partner is kiwi and her father is a very strict (but funny at the same time) English gentleman."

Argentines tend to identify with Europe. "Basically Argentines tend to resemble the French, English, Italians, Spaniards or Germans" Argentines are pressure-prompted (perceiving) "For the 1978 football (soccer world cup) event held in Argentina, literally up until days before these events it looked like chaos but everything was prepared in time and they turned out to be an incredible success. When they want, Argentineans can be very organized and brilliant in their organization when you would think that it is impossible to do whatever the event may be! In many ways, there are a lot of similarities with some Aussies!" (Australians are also perceiving types.)

Argentines are questioning and tough. "The people in my country, if they do not agree with something, they immediately organize themselves to protest. They will fight for a long time if necessary until they find a solution."

Argentines clearly prefer extraversion. "In Argentina we always find any excuse to have friends around, we usually drink 'MATE' (the cheapest drink, and is not alcohol) and talk hours and hours with friends any-day anytime. Sometimes we stay very late at night just talking. If you are going to any city in Argentina you always see people around walking or in cafes and restaurant. In restaurants it is common to see big groups of people. And we love to celebrate all the occasions birthdays especially, marriage, spring day, etc. We don't need to be drunk to have a good night. And the women in my country are more conservative."

"Mendoza is different to some other parts of the country. Mountain people are normally more reserved than people from the plains. The people in Mendoza are reserved with newcomers but are very gregarious and social between their own sub-groups: family, university, clubs, church."

Argentines are expressive and lively: "People have no problem to showing when they are happy or angry. At work if you done something wrong you are usually told what you have done wrong. We kiss each other, a lot of physical contact, even with strangers. In parties people introduce themselves with a kiss, they make you feel comfortable. If you are sitting too far from the group they invite you to join in and make a space for your chair. People speak and laugh loud. Loud people are socially accepted."

MIDDLE EAST

Israel is ESTP:

Clear				Slight				Clear
I				░	░	░		E
N				░				S
F				░				T
P		░	░					J

Israeli culture also is imaginative (N), original (N), empathic (F), compassionate (F), early starting (P).

One Israeli recommended "an excellent novel written by Donna Rosenthal. Her book, *The Israelis*, gives a really interesting sociological perspective on the people of Israel."

"I feel Israelis tend to adjust and fit in almost anywhere, but maybe there are closer feelings to other warm countries. Countries such as India and Brazil and others in their region that enjoy warm climates, tend to have a more open and friendly attitude that Israelis generally to connect with." They are adaptable, perceiving, thinkers that also have a preference for being personable like the Brazilians. Israelis have a secondary preference for thinking and questioning. "Discussion in a loud voice is a way of life. Israelis thrive on it."

Israeli culture favors extraversion and gregarious. "These traits are very much the Mediterranean and Middle-Eastern mentality." Israel is foremost extraverted sensing. They have a "live life to the fullest mentality. Tomorrow we could be at war." They are original and traditional: "of the secular population, yes, not the religious/Orthodox." Israelis are casual "people don't dress up for anything and are very spontaneous-just try to get someone to come on time."

Iraq is ESTP:

Clear				Slight			Clear
I				░	░		E
N				░			S
F				░	░	░	T
P		░	░				J

Iraqi culture also is contained (I), abstract (N), imaginative (N), and early starting (J).

I interviewed a dark-haired, smoothed-skin man from northern Iraq. He was an Arab from Mosul City in the Ninevah Province. The sanctions and war were heavy on his heart and his people. The legacy of the hardship caused by the USA didn't stop with the war; he was also stranded in America by United States Agency for International Development (USAID). He came over in September 2004 on a project funded by USAID (to the University of Hawaii) to get his Ph.D. in agriculture. USAID turned its focus away from education and the project lost funding after a year. UH offered him a six month research internship with the remaining funding. USAID had ended his project so his advisor also abandoned him. He couldn't finish his degree and didn't know what to do. He even had thoughts of trying to get refugee status to try to finish his degree.

"Geographically Iraq is mountainous in the north, flat in the middle and has lakes in the south." There are two ethnic groups: Arabic (80%) and Kurdish (20%). He said, "Since the 1970s, Iraqis have faced continuous problems and the country was only stable in 1988 and 1989." He read that, "If you want to destroy a culture give it four years of bad conditions, and that it takes ten times this amount of time (4x10 or two generations) of good conditions for the culture to return back to the way it was. This will be the case with Iraq."

"There is no health or security for Iraqis. The sanctions took away health and it is dangerous outside on the street. The level of suffering has not changed in Iraq—just who is in and who is out. It is the same as before but as they say with a different mask or face. Salaries have increased but so have prices. I was making $25 a month as a professor before the war and now the pay is $300 a month but prices have risen five to eight times."

Iraqis are easier to know (extraversion) but like to have a private personal life (introversion). He reported the Iraqis as sensing types that prefer tradition. He also pointed out, "the word original is like traditional" (even though they are opposite facets). We think of original as something that isn't an imitation or something new but he saw in the context that it is something that "comes from the origin" or an earlier stage just like tradition.

Iraqi culture prefers thinking types but is split between logical and empathic. "There is a large uneducated majority that believes only in themselves." The educated majority believe in being logical. "What is good for the community is more logical. The uneducated majority is the result of the sanctions. People have limited income so they leave school to go to work. They find work wherever they can even on the street."

About the tough facet of thinking he said, "Life is hard in Iraq. The climate is an example of the hard life. The winter is zero degrees Celsius and the summer is fifty degrees Celsius. Iraqis have a saying 'don't have guts' which means they have a limit. They cannot tolerate too many questions and discussion only up to a certain point."

Iraqi culture prefers perceiving types. "They adapt to the bad conditions around them (relating to work, housing and food). They don't work to change the bad conditions around themselves. Their lives are routine because of the hardship. Just going to work and coming back home and not even enjoying their food, but really the people prefer and desire variety." His last remark was, "please be honest in your writing."

Pakistan is ESTP:

Clear				Slight			Clear
I				░	░		E
N				░			S
F				░	░		T
P	░	░					J

Pakistani culture also is intimate (I), imaginative (N), theoretical (N), compassionate (F), and systematic (J).

EUROPE

Albania is ESTP:

Clear				Slight			Clear
I				░	░	░	E
N				░			S
F				░			T
P	░	░					J

Albanian culture also is imaginative (N), original (N), empathic (F), and compassionate (F).

The Albanians prefer extroversion and are sociable. "Partially due to communism, partially due to Mediterranean culture, Albanians are open and sociable." They are warm and expressive. "This also is typical for the Balkans and Mediterraneans. To an unknown person, people are often open, and easy-to-know, since they think it could turn out to be a good relation, or they do not want to be indifferent, which is partially seen as negative." They are lively and "possibly has also to do with climate and much sun during the whole year. Should be a significant positive correlation between the latter and the energy people reflect in their daily life, I expect."

Sensing types are practical and stick to the facts. "Life itself is very simple in Albania, or at least used to be, and people lived by facts." As sensing types they can be traditional. "Typical for Albania is the respect for elderly people, if one (except kids) enters the room, all the present people stand for example, similar with teachers in the classroom, etc. Typical also is the respect for the guest, and the honour related to that. It is usual (and actually it was many years ago too) that friends meet very often during the week (both women and men). This is not common in Switzerland for instance. Meetings are basically in cafes or other similar places. A strong fact is that, only one pays, and not every body for itself. Next time pays possibly the other, and so on. I have often problems with this tradition, since the friends 'do not let me pay'. I am a guest every time I go back. I can pay if they come to Switzerland, which they basically cannot do due to visa problems. Guests typically do not pay or 'are not allowed to pay' as they say. Actually, the problem I have relates to the little money they have, but still they have their honour, and respect towards others."

"Another example: we had some guests from Sweden back in 1994. We tried to treat them as guest and bought some 'expensive' things and good food. It was around half of a monthly salary (at that time). One of Swedes told me, 'You do not seem to be poor. You eat basically better then we do'. Well, we borrowed the money just for the guest. And we would not eat that way in our daily life. A strong characteristic I thing of Albanian culture is the willingness to sacrifice, being this in the family between mother and children, within groups of friends, parents and children (adult ones) and so on."

Albanians have learned to be resourceful (intuition) and create new and unusual solutions, "maybe also due to too much improvisation needed to overcome difficulties in life. A broken clock, or an instrument, people would try to repair with different 'small invention', whereas in other modern countries there is no need for improvisation and novelty in the everyday life. A funny example, we did not have proper pots for washing. People cut the coca-cola bottles and used them instead. Or how to boil water (in student dormitories), if one did not have a proper boiler, just electrolyze water in two metallic bins (from conserved food), etc." As extraverted sensors "improvisation brings novelty, and we to seek novelty."

Also, as extraverted sensors they are nonconforming and unique. "There was no 'formatting' process in Albania as happened in most of great countries. Great authors and writers have formatted the language, the way people express, and to some extend the way people think, in fact the latter is very much due to press. This process has not happened in Albania. Everyone thinks in his own way. There are different popular sayings, and if you have 10 Albanians they will make up 100 different opinions." Albanians are perceivers: "People do not have agenda, or at least I have never seen one that has or had!!"

Albanians secondary preference is for thinking, they are critical and want proof. "People tend not to trust, or trust less what the media brings—the opposite of western countries. It also is attributed to the communist system, which 'lied' too long, making people increasingly skeptical." They are tough, which "can be said for a 'man/macho' society like the present in Albania. A tender man is often called 'gay', which is too offensive. Men should be tough and firm. Women are basically ends-oriented, one cannot have a girlfriend, without her thinking she will eventually be his wife."

They also have a feeling types sense of loyalty. "Loyalty has also to do with honour. The man should have an honour, and often it is measured by loyalty. Different from western cultures, honour is a characteristic for every man, and they should be honoured, and enjoy acceptance (which comes from certain attributes). Loyalty is a prerequisite also for being accepted."

Czech Republic is ESTP:

Clear				Slight			Clear
I				▓	▓		E
N				▓	▓	▓	S
F				▓			T
P		▓	▓				J

Czech culture also is intimate (I), imaginative (N), accommodating (F), and accepting (F).

Czech was a mixed bag of responses. The ethnic groups in the Czech Republic are: Czech (90.4%), Moravian (3.7%), Slovak (1.9%), Polish (0.5%), German (0.4%), etc. Czech's neighbors are Slovakia (ISFP), Poland (ISTP), Germany (ISTJ), and Austria (ESTJ). Several responses resembled the neighboring country types.

According to a 2001 census, 59% of the country is atheist, non-believer or non-organized believer, 26.8% Catholic and 2.5% Protestant. The most concentrated linguistic minority in the Czech Republic are ethnic Poles, historically the majority, and today constituting between 10 and 45% of the population, in the Český Těšín district.

Czechs slightly prefer extraversion. "Czechs are usually very open-minded especially after drinking beer, watching football or ice hockey. On the other hand, this openness is limited with regards to our intimate life. After living forty years under communism we do not like anybody to penetrate into our private life. We had enough with the secret police and its every day spying procedures. The character of the Czechs is active, realistic, practical, inquisitive, moderate, placid, critical, self-critical, and language talented."

Iceland is ESTP:

Clear				Slight				Clear
I				▓	▓	▓		E
N				▓	▓			S
F				▓				T
P		▓	▓					J

Icelandic culture also is contained/controlled (I), original/unconventional (N), and planful (J).

"It is important to note that Iceland is a young country, geologically (created through volcanic activity), historically (first settler arrived in 874 AD to be followed by larger groups at the beginning of the 900s), and demographically (66% of Icelanders are between the ages of 15 and 64. The elderly are just under 12% of the population). As a country we came out of poverty only in the mid 1960s but are incredibly active in international investments today. Our traditional craftspeople are well recognized in the folk arts movements; and our spatial and building architects are well received in modern European circles. Icelandic companies employ more people in the UK than Swiss companies (Iceland's population is 300,000. Switzerland's is 7.45 millions) We have one the highest standards (and costs) of living in the world... and this has been based on (good) old-fashioned hard work ethics."

ESTPs are like to take action and seek out excitement. "We have a social inclination to 'work hard and play hard'. We work among the longest hours per week in the OECD (overtime payments pay for our excesses!) yet we are renowned for our all-night partying."

Icelanders as extraverted sensors "seek novelty (enquiring—but still act sensibly)." Icelanders are realists yet open to the new and unusual. They "trust experience (but still use imagination and creativity). Imaginative yet efficient is a key word here. Innovation is embraced but efficiency is expected as a result from it! Most superiors and colleagues will be happy to discuss new and innovative ideas with you and to try them out if they are deemed good. We are inventive—but still respect tradition. We respect tradition, hard work, history and culture: yet we embrace all things modern and efficient (to save labour—not due to laziness, but due to very low unemployment rates)."

Icelanders describe themselves as extraverts. "Talks with ones colleagues by the coffee machine is an essential part of the day." Yet, they also like to be private and reflective at times. "We are social—but have time to reflect. We are introspective—but remember to laugh and have fun. Icelanders generally have a close knit group of friends and often do not feel the need to seek out new people in their group. You can become friends with us though—it just takes a little longer! Do not begin by sharing intimate stories of your lives but begin with general chit-chat. We have our introverts, intellectuals and thinkers (internationally known writers, composers, painters, sculptors, theoreticians...) and yet we have our outgoing performers too (Björk, Silvia Nott...)"

Lastly, Icelanders are perceiving types, "Things like timing and order are not valued very much by Icelanders. It is generally expected to be 10-20 minutes late unless there is a formal meeting (but then the boss would most likely be late himself even if the little people would show up on time). Dress code is not strictly adhered to in a corporate setting and jeans would not be frowned upon." The one exception is they "make firm plans (yet still flexible, can go with the flow)"

"This mix might not set us apart from the rest of the world, but we are happy to live on that bit of the globe that is left to us."

17

ISFJ—Introverted Sensing plus Extraverted Feeling

The next two chapters are about the introverted sensing mental process. ISFJs and ISTJs prefer to use introverted sensing the majority of the time. Their second choice, in the case of the ISFJ, would be extraverted feeling, and for the ISTJ extraverted thinking.

ISFJs use introverted sensing and have a secondary preference for extraverted feeling. We all use introverted sensing when we relate the here-and-now with our past experiences. However, the ISFJ uses it more and is likely to be better at it than other types. Introverted sensing is what ISFJs use in their inner, private world so it's difficult to observe in their actions or words. ISFJs second preference is for extraverted feeling. Extraverted feeling types care-take others and strive for harmony in relationships. ISFJs use extraverted feeling in the outer world and for interactions with others.

Special Aspects of Introverted Sensing

Déjà vu is the French word for 'already seen.' It is the feeling that you have already experienced something in the present situation. Introverted sensing is similar to *déjà vu*—you are reliving a previous experience in the present moment. Something in the present situation has triggered a recollection of a similar situation. Introverted sensors have a talent and greater accuracy for saying 'this is that' or 'this is equal to that'.

Sometimes an introverted sensing type has an association and has to think about where it came from. My introverted sensing wife heard the song lyric "it's too late baby" and immediately said she wants to go to Honmoku (a trendy city in Yokohama, Japan). I asked why and she said, "Just because." But then she thought about it for a minute and realized that the song was used in a TV drama that took place in Honmoku.

Sensing types can be like intuitive types and make a mental leap without knowing steps they took in between. For a sensing type, it's like skipping a rock across the surface of a lake. The rock is the object in the present and the splashes are the sequence of associations triggered by it. The associations don't make sense to the outside observer until the ripples of explanation have spread out. The sensor has to explain all the connections between their unique past experiences before the observer can understand the process that flashed momentarily in their mind.

An intuitive makes leaps into the future whereas the introverted sensor makes leaps into the past. An introverted sensing type can tell events that have happened in the past without actually having seen them. They see something and automatically think about how events transpired up to this point to make that something in the state it is right now. Introverted sensors (like all other types) tend to think everyone thinks like them. My wife thought everyone would have the same association or make an obvious conclusion of what might have happened in the past up to this point. That isn't the case. We all make projections of past events but not with the frequency or expertise an introverted sensing type does.

Introverted sensing and introverted intuitive types have flashes of images in their brain. My Japanese wife remembers English numbers better if she sees the number rather than hears it. She will see the number 45 and someone will tell her the number 46. She will keep repeating the number 46 to herself, but when she goes to write it, she writes 45. Japanese learn how to read and write thousands of complex Chinese characters called Kanji. My wife speculates that Japanese are trained to see kanji so this might be part of the reason her seeing something is so much stronger than hearing it.

One professor of psychology and MBTI expert, Bernie Ostrowski, thinks memory is solely a function of sensing. Some introverted sensors claim to have photographic memory. One introverted sensing (ISTJ) secretary said she remembers where things were filed by using her photographic memory. My introverted sensing wife doesn't want to remember all these small details (especially bad memories) but her brain does it anyway.

ASIA

Japan is ISFJ:

Clear				Slight			Clear
I	▓	▓	▓				E
N				▓			S
F			▓				T
P				▓	▓	▓	J

Japanese culture also is gregarious (E), abstract (N), theoretical (N), logical (T), reasonable (T), and pressure-prompted (P). (The end of Chapter 2 has a decription of each facet.)

The Japanese believe that *nareru to ski ni naru*—you can like anything if you become familiar and accustomed to it. The introverted sensing country type doesn't want to break with the tried and true and with their understanding of the world. Japanese are conventional and value tradition. For example, there are the traditional roles of men and women, respecting the elderly, respecting wisdom and experience, taking the proper course of action, following the rules, etc.

ISFJs have a concern for the welfare of others. However, their desire to protect people's health can be constrained by their introverted sensing preference. Japan has a national health care system that pays for births but in a conservative traditional manner they do not pay for cutting edge medicine like heart surgery. Japanese who want heart surgery have to come to USA where cutting edge medicine is available. Introverted sensors like to stick to the tried and true and avoid the unknown. They generally don't like change and are frequently comparing today with the past. They live their lives by looking to the past.

The USA country type is ESTJ—extraverted thinking with a secondary preference for introverted sensing. Like the Japanese, Americans have a preference for introverted sensing—albeit a weaker one. Japanese prefer tradition, which is a characteristic of introverted sensing. The American country type is introverted sensing but has a preference for being original (the opposite of traditional). Americans prefer original, different, new and unusual ideas. If Americans were intuitive (the opposite of sensing) they would love ideas just for the sake of discussion. Americans are introverted sensing which means new ideas must have a practical application. Therefore, cutting edge medical procedures (new and untested ideas) are found in the USA but not in Japan.

Japanese don't like unexpected change (that they have no frame of reference for) but they love change that is an improvement on the old or a variation of a on something they already know. The Japanese failed to cope with the Kobe disaster because they didn't have anything to relate it to in their experience and they are not good at making a quick decision. They aren't good at reacting spontaneously, getting up on a moments notice and taking action. However they love familiar change. Something they can compare the old with the new and appreciate or despise it accordingly. As introverted sensing types they are very detail oriented and can perfect manufacturing processes. They like to compare the new with the old and see improvements in the product and process. For example, they continue to perfect the process of building computers, electronics and cars.

Introverted sensing types are good at buying and selling goods, and making goods from raw materials. Japanese television shows like *Soka ga Shiritai* constantly feature woodworkers, metalworkers, pen makers, umbrella makers, lantern makers, shoemakers, sushi chefs, fishermen, farmers, ramen and soba chefs, etc. Even in making foods like soba noodles, the process and perfection of the production is glorified more so than the art of cooking.

Extraverted Feeling

Japanese ISFJ culture is accommodating and accepting of others and through this builds a system of trust and belonging. Extraverted feeling types are great social cooperators and they seek harmony through finding out what everyone in the group thinks or feels and trying to develop consensus before making a decision.

Japanese make their company decisions based on *nemawashi*— going around and feeling out everyone's opinion first and making accommodations for opposing opinions. They strive for harmony by getting everyone to agree on a new idea before making a decision to implement the new idea; as a result they take longer to make decisions.

The Japanese are living proof that feeling types base decisions and actions on complex and sometimes conflicting values that don't always make logical sense. Extroverted feeling bases decisions on social values and introverted feeling bases them on inner values. Introverted feeling types like to keep their options open and information coming in, as a result they are open to changing decisions. Extraverted feeling types like to have things decided. Therefore, once the Japanese have made a decision that is fair and harmonious it will not be changed.

Introverted Sensing plus Extraverted Feeling

Introverted sensing types seek efficiency and like to see new improvements in an old process or product. When introverted sensing Japanese buy items (houses, cosmetics, etc.) they tend to think to themselves that 'if it was this way or that way' it would be so much better. New products are constantly rolled out, whether technology, home design or just easier to use mop for the home. Japanese also have a penchant for modifying American technology (cars, cell phones, cosmetics etc) and making it better.

ISFJs have extraverted feeling preference for being accommodating and sensitive to the needs of people. Therefore, Japanese design their homes for efficiency by making everything closer or in the right place which equals less walking distance. Introverted sensing provides the drive for efficiency and extraverted feeling inspires human-centered technology.

Japanese preference for extraverted feeling can be compared to Americans preference for extraverted thinking. Japanese extraverted feeling is anchored by introverted sensory. Japanese consumer products reflect their attention to human considerations. In the USA bottom line economics win out over the feeling preference for human convenience. For example, all Japanese cars have a rain shield wrapping around the top of all the windows. This way you can still roll the window down a little and rain won't come inside. American cars don't usually have this as a standard feature. It is the extraverted feeling culture that makes human comfort a priority and extraverted thinking culture that sees it as an unnecessary expense.

Another example is the USA still doesn't have remote control lights in the bedroom and Japan has for years. Japanese technological innovations are human centered like an electronically warmed toilet seat on a cold evening or small electronic devices that emit an odor that keeps the mosquitoes away.

Japan may not have cutting edge medical technology but they have embraced improvements in the telephone. Cell phone technology was much more advanced and widely used in Japan before the USA caught on. Japanese were using the ultra-light compact cell phone a couple years before California (and California was a couple years before Colorado). When the Japanese see an improvement they like sometimes the whole country switches overnight. They continue to stay ahead of the USA in making and converting to new technology that addresses more human needs and comforts.

Lastly, introverted sensing types are thrifty and seek efficiency. Instead of heating a whole bathroom they heat the toilet seat. Instead of heating the whole living room they heat they space under a large floor table covered with a blanket called a *kotatsu*. Everyone sits around the *kotatsu* with his or her bodies under the covers. Not only is it practical but also satisfies the extraverted feeling for belonging and closeness to others.

Introversion

Books about doing business with the Japanese recommend giving Japanese all the information (of the proposal or deal) up front and then giving them a lot of time to make a decision. Introverts need plenty of time to make decisions or even to reply to questions. In business Japanese are also well known for using their introversion to their advantage. They sometimes use delay tactics to force your hand, to see if you are desperate or short on time and they can wait out a better deal.

The Japanese are the classic introverted onlooker and clearly prefer one-on-one communications with one exception, they are gregarious or fond of company. They flock together and have a broad circle of acquaintances (usually schoolmates and co-workers) and join groups.

It is acceptable to be introverted both as a student and as a teacher. It was much easier for me to be an introverted English teacher in Japan because the children were usually quiet and well behaved. There are exceptions to every generalization and I had one kindergarten class that was explosive. I had to keep the action of the lesson rolling non-stop because I had precious few minutes before they were out of their seats or standing on their chairs. However, this was the exception and all of my other classes were very quiet, contained and reserved.

Japanese also have an extravert outlet. They are extraverts when they go to baseball games. But even that extroversion has an introverted sensing or SJ uniformity to it because they all wave noise makers in unison.

Judging

Japanese are judging types and like advanced plans, self-discipline, and being scheduled and orderly. Japanese are huge consumers of life insurance. Americans believe in prevention but Japanese believe in preparation for the worst. The introverted sensing Japanese seek financial security and stability and as judging types make advanced plans.

Japanese take out life insurance policies in case of cancer or anything else that might happen to the father or breadwinner of the family. If you don't have life insurance in Japan you can't get a home loan. If the breadwinner dies the bank isn't forced to foreclose because life insurance covers the mortgage.

The ISFJ Japanese learn whatever is necessary in order to protect their future and build their economy. Japan emulates America as a means of security. Also, their interest in technology is a matter of security. They made the sacrifice necessary to learn technology (like electronics, computer and cars) to build their economy.

ISFJ Japanese are classic stoics. The roots of this can be seen in their religion. Buddhism demands self-sacrifice (a judging trait) and the Japanese are masters of enduring pain and hardship. An example of self-discipline is the huge savings rate (including retirement savings) of the Japanese.

The Japanese have some exceptions when it comes to opposite preferences of judging and perception. The Japanese like to operate by schedules and make advance plans. However, they tend to be pressure-prompted when it comes to getting things done in general.

Horikoshi at the East West Type and Culture conference stated the Japanese "prefer scheduled and spontaneous (they like to have a plan, but don't mind deviating from it)...Japanese place great value on orderliness and formality; however, there is great preference for ambiguity in interpersonal relationships and nonverbal communication." This lack of decisiveness in personal relationships and opportunity for the unexpected when following a plan are both characteristics of perceiving types.

The senses at play

Introverted sensing types enjoy individual or private sensing experiences like taking a bath. For the Japanese the *ofuro* or bath is a central part of the culture. For example, there are more children's toys for the bath sold in Japan than in the USA. Also, they have public baths and hot springs that are a regular vacation spots.

Another example of sensing is the enjoyment of advertising. The Japanese have made advertising a part of their lives and demand more out of advertising. In Japan, there is constantly new and fresh advertising for the senses that plays on nostalgia (introverted sensing looking to the past) and meets human needs (extraverted feeling).

In Japan, there are even TV commercials to promote TV commercials. Enjoy CM (http://www.enjoy-cm.com/) is a TV commercial campaign to encourage Japanese to enjoy and pay attention to TV commercials. My Japanese wife (also an introverted sensing type) asks what is wrong with this? She loves commercials, especially Japanese ones.

The Japanese in a typical sensing fashion, run through celebrities like the snack and ice cream treats found in the convenience store one year but not the next. They're not even satisfied with their monuments and want to see improvements. The landmark Tokyo Tower is a replica of the Eiffel Tower (but taller and painted red). However, they are planning to build a new Tokyo Tower in 2011 that will be even higher (600 meters high).

As an introverted sensing type my wife knew all the candy in the stores before her friends. Her friends would wonder what a certain candy tasted like and she would tell them and they were surprised how many candies that she had experienced. She said new and rare is what is important and not the taste. As a kid she was attracted to American candy because it was different—it didn't necessarily taste better than Japanese candy but it had dark colors and an unusual taste. Her attraction didn't change to clothes when she got older. It is still food, but it spread from American food to international food and the exotic. She even wants to try Rocky Mountain Oysters (bull testicles). Every culture has strange food but it's the introverted sensoing type that seeks it out. They may seem like perverse people but it's really a function of their introverted sensing desire for a new sensory experience.

For the introverted sensing types appearances are important. In the Japanese cartoon, *Crayon Shinchan*, the father gets a designer shirt and the tag in the neck is uncomfortable. Shinchan suggests cutting it out and his father and mother are shocked. They object saying it wouldn't be a designer shirt anymore.

At work

Japanese companies reflect an ISFJ work environment. A new employee at a Japanese company can expect to have a period of six months to a year where they aren't expected to produce but instead just soak up the company environment, get to know their co-workers and begin to feel part of the group.

When I worked at NEC, one of my coworkers was told to learn about Virtual Private Networks (VPNs) and spent a whole year—almost without supervision—just learning on his own. Another friend in Japan started as a Visual Basic computer programmer at a Japanese company. He had six-month period where they didn't ask him to do anything, so he just spent his time learning about programming. This is a stark contrast with the ESTJ American culture where you are expected to be up and running, ready to be productive and performing from day one.

ISFJs love ceremony. I worked for a Japanese commodity broker that had a ceremony each month where all the employees would line up and stand at attention while the president spoke. We finished the meeting by raising our right fists and shouting the company name in unison.

A good example of ISFJs difficulty in making change is the Japanese finance and banking crisis. It took years to make the necessary changes and open the markets. Also, ISFJs like the Japanese tend to avoid high risk investments, ventures, etc.

Bill Bridges described ISFJ companies in his book *The Character of Organizations*, "Although a newcomer may not understand it until too late, there is an invisible credit-and-debit sheet that tracks what you have contributed and what the organization has done for you. People who aren't used to such a system find they have run up some kind of mysterious debt in people's eyes: They seem to owe the company something. And in time, that can be oppressive."

This is a good description of not only the Japanese workplace but of Japanese society in general. For example, the housewives keep notebooks that keep track of what presents and *omiyage* (souvenirs) they have received from other family and friends and make sure they always return the present in like kind and usually of greater value.

Religion

According to Japanophile and MBTI type enthusiast Christopher E. West, the Emperor has never been overthrown in Japan, although at times he had no power. This is a lasting example of an introverted sensors regard for authority and positions of power and the need for tradition and avoiding change.

Introverted sensing types are always looking to their vivid past memories and can see the ideal and how to become the ideal. The ISFJ knows the ideal and feels it's their duty to try hard to live up to it. The ISFJ Japanese looks at history for their ideal culture. The Emperor is an example of looking to the past and comparing it to the present and holding onto the good.

West theorized the reason why Japan has little religious activity (active practice) is because their culture (their rituals and ceremonies) is their religion. Introverted sensing types love rituals and the Japanese have multiple rituals such as words said before and after eating; before entering a house; the ceremony of pouring drinks; and gift giving when visiting or coming back from a trip.

Vietnam is ISFJ:

Clear				Slight			Clear
I	▓	▓	▓				E
N				▓	▓		S
F	▓	▓	▓				T
P				▓	▓		J

Vietnamese culture also is conceptual (N) and emergent (P).

For the extraverted feeling Vietnamese maintaining social harmony is important and this is achieved through self discipline and avoiding conflict. Self discipline is an example of the Vietnamese preference for judging but they also reported that they like to be adaptable and allow things to emerge, which is perceiving.

The Vietnamese are introverts and are self depreciating. Modesty is part of the introverts desire to be quiet and seek the background and the feelings types being tactful.

Like many Asian cultures, the Vietnamese have a sensing types regard for tradition and honoring those that have come before them. Elderly are looked to for direction and shown respect.

Religion in Vietnam is a synthesis of Mahayana Buddhism, Confucianism, and Taoism (called the "triple religion" or *tam giáo*). These are the same religions practiced by the ISFJ Japanese. Vietnamese also believe spirits reside in plants, objects, and natural phenomena. Their belief in harmony and purity is similar to the Shinto religion of the ISFJ Japanese. ISFJs also love ceremony and the Vietnamese and Japanese have endless ceremonies and festivals.

Singapore is ISFJ:

Clear				Slight				Clear
I	▓	▓	▓					E
N				▓	▓	▓		S
F		▓	▓					T
P				▓	▓			J

Singaporean culture also is logical (T), and pressure-prompted (P).

The Singaporean Chinese are ISFJ. Singaporean Chinese account for 76.8% of Singaporeans. Singaporean Malays, who are the indigenous native group of the country, constitute 13.9%, Indian Singaporeans are the third largest ethnic group at 7.9%. I speculate that the Malays and Indians may have a different type; also, because they have a different religion.

More than 40% of Singaporeans profess adherence to Buddhism. The large percentage may be due to a lack of distinction between Taoism and Buddhism. Like the Vietnamese, Taoism, Confucianism, Buddhism, and ancestral worship are merged into one religion by most of the Chinese population. Most Malays are Muslim. Christianity in Singapore consists of Roman Catholicism and various Protestant denominations, and comprises approximately 14% of the population. Other religions include Sikhism, Hinduism and the Baha'i Faith followed mainly by those of Indian descent.

Laos is ISFJ:

Clear				Slight			Clear
I	▓	▓	▓				E
N				▓	▓		S
F	▓	▓	▓				T
P				▓	▓		J

Laotians believe their ancestors speak to them—or they hear their voices. Communication from dead ancestors might be a commonality among ISFJ Asian countries or part of a shared religion.

EUROPE

Latvia is ISFJ:

Clear				Slight			Clear
I	▓	▓	▓				E
N				▓	▓		S
F		▓	▓				T
P				▓	▓		J

Latvian culture also is critical (T) and pressure-prompted (P).

Latvians answers were consistent except for a split between thinking and feeling—with feeling barely winning the majority. One Latvian mentioned the 'siege' of the Germans. Historically, Latvia was both a Swedish (ISFJ) and German (ISTJ) colony so this might explain the split thinking and feeling in the culture. The ethnic groups are: Latvians (58.9%), Russians (29.6%), Belarusians (4.1%), Ukrainians (2.7%), Poles (2.5%), and Lithuanians (1.4%).

Latvian culture is introverting "very northern-like, much cooler than Spanish for example. We are very reserved, it is not easy for us to start a conversation ourselves with foreigners. We prefer to answer the questions, not to ask. It does not mean that we are not interested in other people, just shy. Latvians would not express feelings to anyone, however are very honest." Introverts need time to make up their mind. "We are quite slow to take a decision."

Latvians "live individually and much prefer privacy. I noticed this especially while living here in Ireland; we like to get together but not too often. We are very big individualists. And I also see this from the way Latvians used to build their houses in the 19th- 20th century, not in villages, but far away from each other and preferably windows facing the opposite direction from their neighbours. I'd say we like solitude, but we are also very lively and very energetic, but it does not mean we are looking for spotlight."

Latvians have an introverted sensing work ethic: "We are world-wide-known as being very very hard working. I think very highly of Latvian women, especially who are in their 50s. How much strength they have. There is more than one lady who I have had a privilege to meet, who have brought up 2 or 3 children on their own. From the Irish (western) point of view it might not sound that difficult, but life is so different in Latvia."

Introverted sensors prefer concrete, exact facts, and to be literal in communication. "This comes from Germans, since we have been for so long under their siege. A 'yes' is a yes and a 'no' is a no, unlike the Irish, where a yes is maybe and no is yes etc." Introverted sensors are also not risk takers. "We are not very adventurous."

However, Latvians also have a preference for being intuitive: "because of the way of life, especially during the Soviet era, people are very resourceful—most people have not lost the ability to make something out of nothing. However, we are starting to lose it, for example, our parents know what is wrong with a car when it breaks down and they can in most of the cases repair it at home in their own garage, where as the new generation have no idea and they bring it to a car service (garage)."

Latvians show their thinking preference in their skepticism. A Euro-skeptic is a person who is skeptical of the joining of European economies and powers (European Union). "We are the most Euro-skeptical people amongst the EU nations because we are so critical about ourselves and others. Never satisfied."

Latvians are judging types, but also pressure-prompted. "In 2002, the Latvians won the Eurovision song contest and in 2003 they had to organize the event. Even a week before the event had to take place the location was not even ready build and the Eurovision commission was considering canceling the festival. However in the last days everything was ready and the event was well organized. The same goes for the world championship ice hockey last May in Riga and in November next the NATO summit will be held in Riga."

Norway is ISFJ:

Clear				Slight				Clear
I			▓					E
N				▓	▓			S
F			▓					T
P				▓				J

Norwegian culture also is gregarious (E), active (E), conceptual (N), reasonable (T), questioning (T), and pressure-prompted (P).

The Norwegians reported themselves as ISFJ but a couple people reported ISFP. "The social and work habits of many people in Norway have definitely changed during the past 10-15 years, and are still changing, but you can say that the majority of the population probably have not embraced them yet. There is quite a bit of difference between urban and rural Norway, still, in terms of doing things a certain way. The country as a whole is still more rural than urban in my view." Possibly there is a perceiving/judging difference between rural and urban Norway?

Norwegians are introverted sensing types. "We Norwegians are very stuck on rules. We do not break them—even if common sense should tell us so. Rules are definitely there to be upheld, where the Irish for example have a much more relaxed attitude to rules." Which makes sense because the Irish are clearly perceiving.

The Norwegians are feeling types yet also have a preference for being precise. "Whilst the Irish would tell you 'little lies' to make you feel comfortable, the Norwegians would tell you the unpleasant truth, whether or not asked for it." Which also makes sense because the Irish clearly feeling types who prefer to maintain harmony.

Sweden is ISFJ:

Clear			Slight				Clear
I			▓				E
N				▓	▓		S
F			▓				T
P				▓	▓	▓	J

Swedish culture also is active (E), conceptual or theoretical (N), logical (T), critical (but some say reasonable) (T), and open-ended (P).

Who are Swedes similar to and get along easily with? "Swedes—unsurprisingly—tend to gravitate towards each other. So the first choice would always be: other Swedes! They are also known to be 'the Japanese of Europe', although I doubt that Swedes gel particularly well with Japanese people. I think Swedes in general admire and try to emulate Britons and Americans plus their offshoots the Australians, Canadians, Irish & New Zealanders."

"Sweden is sometimes referred to as the 51st state of America—which is an exaggeration but indicates the pervasive influence that Anglo-Saxon civilisation has had on Sweden since WWII. Swedes tend to identify much less with other Europeans—apart from of course the natural kinship to other Nordic countries Norway, Finland, Denmark and Iceland (although the differences are much more marked than outsider would think). They would perhaps sense some affinity to Dutchmen and to a lesser degree Germans, Austrians, Swiss people."

Swedes reported themselves as clearly sensing and judging types. The Swedish prefer feeling slightly over thinking. The Swedish are similar to the ISFJ Japanese in that they are balanced between thinking and feeling.

One Swedish UH student said northern Sweden is feeling (makes decisions using their heart) and southern is thinking (makes decisions using their head). Another Swede living in Singapore said, "I would say that the further north you go the quieter and more private people tend to get...Again this is a stereotype but there

is some truth to it... The South of Sweden is more densely popu-
lated and historically and geographically as well as culturally closer
to Denmark and the rest of the continent, thus more spontaneous,
talkative. The north more quiet, reflective, contemplating."

Swedes also have an intuitive and thinking side. One student
commented, "The Swedish are very focused on academic partly
because of jobs and partly because achievement is important. There
is a 'Swedish Jealousy' that everyone in Sweden has but no one talks
about. They are always noticing others and trying to one up them
whether its in education or fashion." This sounds a bit like the ISFJ
Japanese obsession with name brand fashions and the importance
that the designer label is showing; also, with the extraverted feeling
desire for social belonging.

The Swedish extraverted feeling can possibly be seen in their
values. "Sweden closes down completely in the summer and we all
disappear to various cottages in the country which lack internet
and telephone and sometimes even running water." Extroverted
feeling types value the ability to separate work and personal life.
Extroverted feeling types also commit to recharging and renewal as
opposed to the American extroverted thinking value of taking all
the stress you can handle.

MIDDLE EAST

Iran is ISFJ:

Clear				Slight			Clear
I							E
N							S
F							T
P							J

Iranian culture also is active (E), enthusiastic (E), tough (T),
casual (P), and pressure-prompted (J).

"I considered the people in my hometown of Zanjan, who are
more reserved. I found it interesting to think that my hometown
people are different, depending if they are behaving inside the fam-

ily or in the public sphere. That is, very different codes of behavior and principles for the personal and collective lives."

My experience with first generation Persians in California was that they were more gregarious, expressive, warm and helping like an extraverted feeling type. ESFJ might fit the American-Persians because one type expert said the people you meet abroad tend to be the extraverts of their country. One Persian said, "In Iran the garden is in front of the house. Americans will let you in the garden but not in the house, Persians are the opposite and welcome you in the house."

18

ISTJ—Introverted Sensing plus Extraverted Thinking

ISTJs use introverted sensing and have a secondary preference for extraverted thinking. We all use introverted sensing when we relate the here-and-now with our past experiences. However, the ISTJ uses it more and is likely to be better at it than other types. Introverted sensing is what ISTJs use in their inner, private world so it's difficult to observe in their actions or words. ISTJs second preference is for extraverted thinking. Extraverted thinking types plan and logically organize projects and activities to achieve a goal. ISTJs use extraverted thinking in the outer world and for interactions with others.

According to MBTI expert Ray Moody, ISTJs have the hardest time adjusting to other cultures (culture shock etc.) I think they also have a hard time adjusting to and accepting people coming into their culture, i.e. new immigrants. Introverted sensing types build a rocklike foundation of internal understanding of the world from their personal experience. When this internal understanding is challenged by the new and the unknown, it's a blow against their foundation. Therefore, when they encounter an immigrant for the first time, they may have a negative reaction because it is something out of the ordinary and requires them to restructure their internal foundation or way of doing things and reacting.

ISTJs countries are only in Europe. I was surprised to get so many replies from Finnish, Estonians, Czechs and Swiss. One could speculate that people from ISTJ cultures are a bit more dependable.

Finnish and Estonian societies are of similar origin. They are thinkers yet both cultures have an accommodating, sympathetic side, which may be a another reason they were so helpful with my research.

EUROPE

Finland is ISTJ:

Clear				Slight			Clear
I	░	░	░				E
N				░	░		S
F				░	░		T
P				░	░	░	J

Finnish culture also is original (N) and maybe theoretical (N), and also accommodating (F). (The end of Chapter 2 has a decription of each facet.)

"Even if Finns are not a completely homogenous group, the country's population is just 1/60 of the US population, so Finnish culture can be defined a little easier than American Culture."

The Finns have an ISTJ work ethic. "Finland has a long history of having to deal with their much larger Eastern neighbour, whilst still retaining their independence. During the Winter and Continuation Wars (Finland's WWII), their guts and determination, together with the other qualities mentioned, became legendary and the legacy of that hard period in their history is still evident in the national psyche."

The Finnish are like many introverted sensors: "In all activity a well thought through approach is most valued. So as long as the presentation or a performance is prepared there is no problem when presenting it." Also as introverted sensors have a preference for being concrete and realistic and as a result value security.

"In Finland, security is a very important common value and need both for young people and for elder people. This is an important and unfortunate phenomenon because that is why Finnish people are not very entrepreneurial." (Routamaa, 2006 Type and Culture Conference).

However, Finnish also have a preference for the intuitive characteristic of new and original. One Finn felt, "innovation is one of Finland's strengths. New waves in the music industry are an example of this." Another person commented that although the Finnish tend to be realistic given its "reputation for its excellent education and for being the most competitive of economies", there are also exceptions where they can be inventive and innovative, for example, the 'Nokia experience'. "Finns are very imaginative in finding innovative ways for efficiency. And we are encouraged to that in all levels. All practical is based on a concept but the practical work still gets done. At the same time as Finns are innovative we also value moderation and stability in all actions."

Finnish as introverts are reserved and hard to get know whether socially or in business. One Finn commented, "One-to one conversations are considered confidential. Trust is important overall. It takes time to get to know us, but when you do, you get friends for life." Also as introverts the Finnish have a preference for the quiet and solitude. "This must be because of the culture overall and long physical distances geographically. People enjoy spending time in cottages in the countryside. There's also a saying *vaikeneminen on kultaa* (Silence is gold)." The Finns traditionally retreat to their summer cottages for a few weeks during the short summer they experience. These cottages are generally remote and by a lake. There they walk in the woods, pick berries, take saunas, commune with nature and 'contemplate the meaning of life'."

There are exceptions to being introvert too: "As people are being introduced they also introduce others. It would not be polite not to introduce others. On the other hand you are not expected to memorize people's names at once."

Finnish are extraverted thinking types and are especially akin to being principle centered. For example, in Finland verbal agreements are valid and should be followed. Finns are "matter-of-fact, down to earth logical. Not very superstitious. Everything is driven by rational thinking and factuality."

Finns are slightly prefer thinking so they also show their feeling side. They tend be accommodating and have a compassionate side which shows in business. As one Finn put it, "Finns are loyal once they build a proper connection. As you get to know a person they are very genuine and open."

Lastly, Finns are systematic, planful and methodical. Finns "hold on to timetables, plans, and agreements." And in business, time-tables are followed. They feel "that's why results are gained and progress happens." Finns start things early, "because of the habit of planning. There's a saying *hyvin suunniteltu on puoliksi tehty* (Well planned is half done)."

Estonia is ISTJ:

Clear				Slight			Clear
I	▓	▓	▓				E
N				▓	▓		S
F				▓	▓	▓	T
P				▓	▓	▓	J

Estonia borders Russia and the Gulf of Finland. "Estonians and Russians are indeed very different. Russians are Slavs, Estonians, on the other hand, are Finno-Ugric people and are close in their temperament and especially language to Finns. As always, everything depends on a person and not all Estonians are alike. There are all kinds of people with all kinds of temperaments and ideals. In general, Estonians are quiet, private and like to keep to themselves. An old people's saying describes us pretty well: 'Speaking–silver, silence–gold'"

One Estonian explained their introversion: "Estonians are low-key, they don't show their feelings or let you know what they are thinking, no emotions are showed. They keep distance with strangers. I think this low-key and reserved comes already from old times—Estonians were living far away from each others, middle of nowhere (rounded with big forests) and they had no one to communicate with. So they become more and more closed. Estonians are proud and happy about Estonian things. Being under the Soviet Union, Estonians were not allowed to have such a things (like singing Estonian songs, reading Estonians books). So they have grown like being in the box with no sunshine. Of course the weather (cold and cloudy summer, cold and dark winter) leave its own stamp of being introvert. Estonians seek intimacy because they don't know how to act and communicate being with other people. They are afraid of failing and they afraid of others taunt. They are always onlookers; prefer space because they are introverts. You don't see never-ever a sober Estonian starting a social acting (like dancing or singing). Reading and writing–they like to think a lot and that's why they need space and like solitude."

Another Estonian explained their introversion: "Anglo-Americans usually start a conversation by 'Hello, I'm David' while Estonians would just say 'Hello!' and introduce themselves only after being asked or after the other person has done so first." Estonians are harder to get to know compared to their neighbors the extra-verted Russians, "The classic example: If there is more than one empty seat on the bus and there's a choice between sitting next to someone or taking one of two empty seats, an Estonian will choose the latter, a Russian the former." Another example: "When students who don't know each other are standing in a hall way waiting for a lecture to start, Estonians usually don't speak to each other or, after a while, start talking to the person next to them (they usually stand further away from each other, as well). Russians, on the other hand, always talk amongst themselves in a group. During and after a lecture or a public performance of some sort, Estonians don't like to ask questions or participate in a discussion. They feel uncomfortable when put in the spotlight, being asked a question in front of the crowd. They like to sit in back rows and corners."

Like many introverted sensing types they look to the past for meaning and find security in traditions. "Estonians love traditions, it's safe and doesn't let them down. Even there come too many different traditions from 'Europe' and from American movies nowadays (to weddings, like throwing and catching the bride bouquet), there is always something from old days tradition." As sensing types they are realistic trust the tried and true: "Estonian students, for example, hardly question what they read or hear from the lecturer. They take it as a matter of fact without analyzing it or trying to figure it out for themselves." Sensing types stick to the facts. "Estonians keep it short and simple! They often give 'yes' and 'no' answers."

Although clearly sensing types they also can be intuitive, "It seems that Estonian higher education, for example, is very theoretical as opposed to American one which is more practical, applied. In Estonian culture (old days), there are lots of symbols which have their own meaning. Estonian old culture has its own gods, fairies, and that's intangible."

Estonians are thinking types, who prefer reason to emotion. "Estonians like the truth and specific facts about a situation. When something happens (a small accident to someone they know, a failure of some sort), Estonians try to find out why it happened and what to do next instead of asking the person if they're OK or bursting into tears and hugs." They can also be critical, "Estonians are a bit suspicious, they don't trust what they hear from the media or some authority, they want proof."

Although Estonians are thinking types they do prefer to be accommodating and seek harmony. They believe "to live peacefully, they need harmony. They have learned to suppress their feelings. They maintain harmony by being calm, even if they might feel otherwise inside. Don't do to others what you don't want to be done to yourself. That's the strategy! While Americans, for example, are very success-oriented from an early age, Estonians are not that competitive. They don't need to be part of a winning sports team in school; they don't need to have a high paid job right after high school. They don't do well in a cut-throat business climate, as they don't like to step on other people."

Like the Finnish, the Estonians are clearing judging types because they like to have things decided, are systematic and desire routine. "If Estonians are decided already, they don't remake it over even if it doesn't suit. They need to be systematic if they want something to work out. They are stubborn. Routine is the only way to live peacefully. Estonians are pretty organized and precise. Estonians like to plan ahead as opposed to being spontaneous. Spaniards are always late, they do things when they feel like it, they can stop what they're doing for hours to chat with a friend. For Estonians, work comes before pleasure, deadlines are important; a professional attitude towards keeping your things in order is valued. Easy does it for Estonians. They like to know what they have to do in advance so they can start planning and work towards their goal steadily and calmly, think things through."

Germany is ISTJ:

Clear				Slight			Clear
I		▓					E
N				▓	▓		S
F				▓	▓		T
P				▓	▓		J

German culture also is gregarious (E) and theoretical (N).

"The neighboring states of Germany, such as Switzerland and Austria, (which are in part also German-speaking countries) resemble Germans to a certain extent. If one has a look at the former territories of Germany, for instance East Prussia (which is now Poland), one might mention certain regions of those countries as well. However, a German who lives in Kiel might get along easier with people from Denmark than with someone who lives in Munich. There are differences within Germany, too. This is perhaps due to the fact that there was no German state per se before the 19th century. Until then 'Germany' consisted of numerous princedoms." One German girl said, "The north isn't different from the south and the east is rapidly becoming like the west. Also you never see East Germans traveling. I don't know why this is."

Germany is a classic example of an ISTJ country, however that is changing. "Since globalization and its repercussions are ubiquitous traditional values are blurring in Germany as well." One German commented "characteristically, I would say Germans tend to be somewhat similar to the Swiss and to Scandinavians in terms of mannerisms and society." They are similar to the Swedish in that prefer sensing but are also theoretical. "One example could be that most of the universities are still focused on theories and don't show their students how real life works or what the theory's limits are."

Sensing types prefer convention and tradition. "The elder people are really conventional. Some still haven't realized that the German Wall doesn't exist anymore. The younger people are different and seek the new. But because the German society is rather old, I put 'Traditional'."

Germans introverted sensing mixed with extraverted thinking creates a preference for precision. "Germans are known for their exactitude and it's true. We love numbers and want to be accurate. It can't be that there is one case/issue/topic not covered by law or regulation."

As thinking types "German people watch their own gain and only sometimes think about the whole picture, e.g. all issues in politics." However, thinking type does not equal unemotional. They have an affective side, German "people are very emotional."

According to a couple of German university students at UH, "Germany's politics are extraverted but its people are introverted." Another person working at a US embassy said, "People seldom offer strangers to sit next to them in a restaurant in case all seats are taken; people would never say 'Make yourself at home' to guests who spend a few days in their home. People don't talk about private topics unless they know the other person well. Germans love to listen, but also love to just watch and they prefer space. They don't say 'hello' if they meet somebody from their company but who they don't work with; in public transportation they like to sit alone and have the seat next to them taken with their own luggage." Despite having a strong preference for introversion, the Germans are also gregarious. "People like to participate in different clubs (sports, books, music, theater) and enjoy events together with others, people like to celebrate with the crowd and hear themselves talk/hold speeches. Germans are always on the run, even retired people never have time."

Germans are the classic judging type. They like structure and order, "e.g. bureaucracy: spent money must be proven and one needs a receipt. Teachers want routine, professors want routine, workers want routine, business men want routine; everybody likes to list tasks and procedures."

Switzerland is ISTJ:

Clear				Slight				Clear

I			░	░				E
N					▓	▓		S
F					▓			T
P				▓	▓	▓		J

Swiss culture also is theoretical (N), accommodating (F), and maybe also empathic (F).

Switzerland consists of four different languistic/cultural areas. The four official languages of Switzerland are German, French, Italian, and Romansh. German native speakers (mostly Swiss German dialects) number about 64% (4.6 million), French are 20% (1.5 million, including some Franco-Provençal dialects), Italian are 7% (0.5 million; including Lombardic dialects), Romansh number less than 1% (35,000).

An Internet article titled *Swiss pride, Swiss posterity* explains there is a 'soft multiculturalism' in Switzerland similar to Canada. "Different cultural communities can 'hear each other's music and taste each other's food, but that's about all.' This buffet-style multiculturalism manages to give voice to each cultural tradition and language group without bringing political considerations."

Swiss type depends on the subculture: Swiss-German, Swiss-French, Swiss-Italian, Romanch. Many Swiss-Germans uniformly reported to be ISTJ. Also a couple Swiss-French proclaimed they were ESFJ and ENFJ. Since both France and Quebec (French Canada) came out intuitive I am guessing the Swiss-French may be ENFJ.

I interviewed a friendly, talkative guy from Geneva who is studying Law at HPU. He had short bleach blonde hair, a diamond earring in his right ear and one through his eyebrow. The following is his perspective as a Swiss (and as a law student) on Hawaii, USA and Europe compared to Switzerland.

"I went to a casual party in Pearl City, Hawaii. There were children running around and I was talking with a friend from France.

A Filipino came up to me, said something about me being/looking gay and hit me on the head with a bottle. The cops asked if I wanted to press charges. I was surprised because in Switzerland it would be automatic." He was put in the position of having to make things possibly even worse for himself. He told the cops, "Just make him pay for my bills and tell me why he hit me." The guy never told him why. He can still press charges but he figured the next time it could be a group of them and they might kill him.

He is shocked at the level of violence in America. "I had friend in Hawaii who has been beaten up several times—one time when he was drunk in front of a Burger King. America is a young country and is like a teenager with its violence and wars. Europe has a long history and has gone through all of that before. European society doesn't tolerate violence or jump into wars it is more civilized."

All the homeless on Fort Street mall in downtown Honolulu shocked him. Introverted sensors like the Swiss believe you must set an example for children to follow and to learn proper socially acceptable behavior. "Kids see the homeless and it sets a bad example. Kids see homelessness as accepted and normal and therefore can more easily become one themselves."

Switzerland prefers thinking but like many European also has a preference for empathy. Feeling types favor values centered on empathy and human considerations over being objectively impersonal. "European countries have social systems that raise the socioeconomic level of everyone so that there is less violence and homeless. In Switzerland even a cashier at a department store gets a living wage. The minimum salary level for all jobs is something like $2500 a month. France is one of the European countries with the most social benefits—even more than the Swiss. Up to 60% of company revenues go to social benefits like the unemployment fund—therefore there are less poor people."

"The schools are free in Switzerland (and many other countries in Europe). Education raises the level of society in general leading to less violence, poor and homeless. In Europe social rights (social benefits) came out of the industrial revolution of the 1800s and this may be why the US has less social benefits because it didn't have an industrial revolution."

The Swiss as ISTJs are judging, pragmatic, traditional and contractual. He was surprised at how fat and badly dressed people in Hawaii were. "In Europe if you are fat and dress bad people judge you fast—they believe clothes reflect the inner person. In Europe there are divisions of people by the clothes they wear. On the other hand, people in Hawaii are friendly, for example, at the bank, whereas in Switzerland it is very businesslike and contractual. The bank ads in Hawaii have a surfer on them or something like that—which is very different from conservative Switzerland. The Swiss are more pragmatic than religious. The church is not so much a part of life. Also, the Swiss are somewhat closed to other cultures, traditional and conservative."

In the introverted sensing cultures like Switzerland it is important to know the rules of society. "In Hawaii (and the US) signs state the laws, e.g. don't litter, no dogs allowed etc. Europe has been a society for hundreds of years so there are no laws written on signs—everyone just knows the rules. Even newspaper vending machines aren't locked like in the US. You could take a paper out without putting money in, however everyone knows the rules of society and still pays the fee."

Although the ISTJ Swiss are contractual they are also accommodating and thus seek balance and harmony. "In Switzerland you can't sue a person for millions like you can in the USA—only for compensation of the extent of injury. He speculates that Americans do this to calm people here—fear of a lawsuit is a deterrent."

19

ENTJ—Extraverted Thinking plus Introverted Intuition

The next two chapters are about the extraverted thinking mental process. ENTJs and ESTJs prefer to use extraverted thinking the majority of the time. Their second choice, in the case of the ENTJ would be introverted intuition, and for the ESTJ introverted sensing.

ENTJs use extraverted thinking and have a secondary preference for introverted intuition. We all use extraverted thinking when we plan and logically organize projects and activities to achieve a goal. However, the ENTJ uses it more and is likely to be better at it than other types. Extraverted thinking is what ENTJs use in the outer world and for interactions with others. ENTJs second preference is for introverted intuition. Introverted intuitive types have occasional flashes of insight or visions into what the future will hold. ENTJs use introverted intuition in their inner, private world so it's difficult to observe in their actions or words.

EUROPE

France is ENTJ:

Clear				Slight				Clear
I				██				E
N			██					S
F				██	██			T
P				██	██			J

French culture also is traditional (S), empathic (F), spontaneous (P), and emergent (P). (The end of Chapter 2 has a decription of each facet.)

For intuitive types, like the French, thoughts are expressed just for the sake of ideas. The French 'rationale' relates to the thinking facets of reason and logic. France's freethinking, arm-chair intellectuals wander from one topic to the next in an exchange of ideas. As ENTJs they expect everyone in both social and work situations to have a well thought out argument, critical feedback or to keep quiet.

Unlike sensing Americans, for the French, ideas don't have to have a practical application. Their propensity for intellectual debate makes their intuition obvious and their stubborn confidence shows their extroverted thinking side. The relationship between the French and Americans sometimes is opinionated, arrogant, extraverted thinking types, each one thinking they are right.

The French are confident in their intellectual theory on how to enjoy and live life. They empathize with creative intuitive types. Several artists and writers became famous after coming to France. The cafes are a place of learning—the abode of philosophers, where famous authors like Hemingway wrote their books. They revere and honor writers by placing them at the top of society as opposed to ESTJ commerce-oriented Americans, which only hold regard for bestsellers.

France is the only ENTJ country in Europe. As ENTJs, France believed in the future vision of a European Union and became one of the leaders in the push towards the goal of integration of Europe. Revolution and riots are part of Frances history and modern day, and in some way revered by the ENTJ French. Yet, the French penchant for risk avoidance is evidence of their judging preference. The ENTP likes to gamble it all on a concept but the ENTJ takes more careful risks. Although judging types, the French can sometimes show up late like a perceiving type.

Unlike their English neighbors, the French, as ENTJs, don't beat around the bush for the sake of harmony. As challenging, thinking types the French look you in the eye, use direct communication and don't worry if this makes them unpopular. The French are thinking types yet also have a preference for being empathic. Empathic is the opposite facet of logical and is about being personal as opposed to impersonal. Sometimes an action or decision can be based on emotion. For the French if you get your emotions involved then it seems like you are really getting involved—on a personal level—and if its personal than you are more committed.

MIDDLE EAST

Jordan is ENTJ:

Clear				Slight				Clear
I				███	███	███		E
N			███					S
F				███				T
P				███	███			J

Jordanian culture also is traditional (S) and empathic (F).

Jordanians are split between sensing and intuition and like the French also prefer to be traditional and empathic.

20

ESTJ—Extraverted Thinking plus Introverted Sensing

ESTJs use extraverted thinking and have a secondary preference for introverted sensing. We all use extraverted thinking when we plan and logically organize projects and activities to achieve a goal. However, the ESTJ uses it more and is likely to be better at it than other types. Extraverted thinking is what ESTJs use in the outer world and for interactions with others. ESTJs second preference is for introverted sensing. Introverted sensors relate the here-and-now with their past experiences. ESTJs use introverted sensing in their inner, private world so it's difficult to observe in their actions or words.

If you look at an announcement for a corporate job opening in the US, it's amusing how many times the job description fits ESTJs, for example, extraverted thinking activities like coordinate, prioritize, organize, plan, schedule, etc. Another example is my ESTJ brother. He is an entrepreneur who outlines a business plan, arranges for funding and organizes management. Of course there is the financial reward but his real joy and passion is in seeing the plan come together and reaching completion. As judging types they like to have closure and for things be decided and completed.

Extraverted feeling types, on the other hand, like to be organized but with a feeling twist. For example, if there is a bag of Halloween candy, you could organize it by all the different kinds of candy, but a feeling type would think about organizing the candy so that each child can get one of each kind of candy.

Extraverted thinking types don't have this feeling twist. According to Otto Kroeger in his book *Type Talk*, ESTJs make the most racist and sexist jokes. This may be why American culture still has some hard lessons to learn about respecting and rewarding those that differ individually and culturally.

Besides the USA and Australia (both originally colonies of ESTJ England), I have found ESTJs and ISTJs are all European countries. The ESTJ American, English and Dutch have obvious differences. The English are more contained, accommodating or indirect whereas the Dutch and Americans are not. The English clearly prefer order and tradition whereas the Dutch and Americans prefer to be unconventional and casual. The Dutch may be more similar to the Americans than the English but the Dutch are obviously empathic with their concern for the welfare of others, whereas Americans tend to be logical and impersonal.

All of these ESTJ countries have subtle differences in preferences. This is the power of applying the twenty facets to a culture instead of just a four-letter type. We know these cultures are not the same and the facets clarify exactly where they are different.

NORTH AMERICA

USA is ESTJ:

Clear				Slight			Clear
I							E
N							S
F							T
P							J

American culture also is original (N), tolerant (part of the accepting facet of feeling), casual (P), and open-ended (P). (The end of Chapter 2 has a decription of each facet.)

Americans from the east-coast, west-coast and mid-west commented on US culture. One of my family members in Colorado reported American culture as ESTJ and commented, "It made me feel like we live in a pretty cold country. I was reminded of the expression 'We are a nation of laws' that politicians frequently state." One American INTJ said, "being impersonal is the only way to be"—and he wasn't joking. Extraverted thinking types like the establishment of order and logic that laws provide, despite the obvious disregard for the human side of the equation. This also is the reason for the contractual nature of American society.

American thinking preference is seen in its love of competition in sports and business. Americans are taught to be "RAM tough" and be willing to get in a fight or go to war to prove we ain't gonna be kicked around. Individuals are responsible for succeeding on their own, and the homeless are just people who don't want to work. Americans have to take as much stress as it takes to succeed. One Australian commented after visiting New York, "What's the problem with Americans? Why are they so uptight?"

One American embassy employee replied: "As Embassy staff it wouldn't be appropriate for us to convey our personal feelings." This is classic extraverted thinking—feelings are not appropriate. As a thinking type, American culture does not prefer the accommo-

dating facet of feeling. For example, I received almost four hundred responses from more than a hundred and fifteen countries. I didn't receive a single response from an American embassy about American culture.

American diplomats are instructed to protect and promote American interests, i.e. economical and political, instead of creating international understanding and building bridges of trust. As an extraverted thinking country, US diplomacy and international relations is about power, money and spreading American intellectual theories of how the rest of the world should live. American politicians have even talked about merging the Foreign Service (the diplomatic staff of the embassies) with the military.

Intellectual Theory

American extraverted thinking culture is ends-oriented, and develops 'mechanisms' for dealing with and solving problems. They expect everyone to fit in and be productive. Extraverted thinking types have principles and laws they live by and build an intellectual theory of logical organization of the world. This theory guides their personal actions and interactions with others. They personally believe and follow their theory and believe the rest of the world should too. America has confidence in its intellectual theory of how the world should be like America and tries to aggressively 'organize' the world.

However, the more Americans understand the different strengths of other cultures, the less biased we will be and our intellectual theory can be reorganized to reflect a world view instead of a nationalistic or type-centric one. Also, American ESTJ culture doesn't fit every individual living in it nor many of its subcultures. The Hawaiian, Indian, Hispanic and Black subcultures are very different from ESTJ American culture.

The violence done to other cultures is obvious, for example, the theft of the Hawaiians' land and their culture by the missionaries and the capitalists with their intellectual formula of property ownership. Even today, Americans continue corporate globalization and forceful democratization (i.e. 'live free or die') of the world.

Democracy is a feeling based system (harmony, consensus, tolerance, etc.) but capitalism is based on the thinking logic of economics—one that doesn't have human considerations. On the white horse of democracy is the dark rider of capitalism.

Lack of Feeling

ESTJs can be blind to other points of view. Americans fail to understand and embrace other countries and cultures. Several countries have working holiday visa that allow an exchange of workers from different countries. For example, Japan has working holiday agreements with seven countries: Korea, Australia, England, France, Germany, New Zealand, and Canada. The US has a major interest in all these countries yet does not support a working holiday visa program with them. When I worked in Japan, I had the pleasure of meeting people from these very countries because they were in Japan on working holiday visas.

Americans, as thinking types, have a tendency to be challenging and competitive, yet may occasionally prefer harmony. "I am thinking political examples here. We love to observe debate, but when it comes down to it we seem to prefer harmony as evidenced by the lack of efficacy in negative campaigns. As a culture, we prefer the positive while having a morbid sense of curiosity for the Jerry Springer-type of entertainment."

Americans are thinking types yet may feign acceptance and tolerance in some circumstances. "I think the U.S. is a troublesome little fellow to try and analyze as a culture because what we value based on our actions is so very different based on what we claim to hold important. I don't think we are actually very accepting, but that with political correctness and other social pressures people keep some judgments to themselves more than they would. Its like a form of cognitive dissonance since we are really rather judgmental, but have decided that we should not be which likely results in more than a little self-flagellation."

Introverted Sensing

American culture is an extraverted thinking culture but also has a secondary preference for introverted sensing. Introverted sensing types are interested in commerce. The USA is a consumer society and Americans like commercials, advertising, promotions, sales, etc. The TV infomercials are filled with get-rich, start-your-own-business, and home business programs like how to flip properties, medical billing from home, multi-level marketing, etc.

"I heard someone once say that 'English is the language of commerce'. Similarly, I think we are a nation of commerce. I mean, why do so many people want to come here? Sure there is the freedom issue, but wouldn't you agree, its mostly for the money."

Misinformation

One person traveled to China and commented on how many countries have technological advancements that aren't in the USA. There is a misconception that the USA is the most technologically advanced country. For example, compared to the US, people living in countries like Japan and Korea can get a hundred times faster high-speed Internet access in their homes. One American attended an European conference on digital resources and was surprised at how advanced the Europeans were. She returned home to report what she had learned, but found her American co-workers weren't interested. They were determined to believe that the Europeans couldn't possibly know more than Americans about technology.

Technological advancements are easier to see than social differences. There also is the American misconception that the US is the most socially advanced society. Yet, when you live in other countries you find there are many different ways of life that are superior to American ways. Quality of life is better through the choices a society makes. These choices are the result of the culture type. A society that is a thinking culture will make very different choices from a feeling culture.

The American government doesn't publish statistics on where Americans emigrate to, but there are loads of statistics on immigrants coming to the USA. It's as if subconsciously Americans believe people only want to come the USA and no American would want to leave it. But Americans do leave the USA, for social, cultural and other reasons.

Canada (a feeling type culture) has received a large number of American immigrants, especially after President Bush was re-elected. One Ontario Canadian commented, "Americans are immigrating to Canada for the better quality of life, national healthcare, and higher minimum wage but the Canadian doctors are moving to the USA because they can make more money." One Australian joked that the biggest illegal immigration problem they have is with Americans.

Extraversion

Americans have a clear preference for extraversion. "It is considered impolite not to introduce people. This may be more tied to education level and the circles an individual run in for all I know." Americans are gregarious and join groups. "Heck, MySpace, MSN Spaces, and Friendster are great technology examples of this attitude." American extraverts also have a fondness for 'conferences' of all kinds.

Americans are not introverted or intuitive. Extraverts tend to get impatient working on a project for a long time. "I also tend to equate scholarly or idea oriented as patient since working through ideas or researching something just plain takes time." Americans as sensing types are realistic, sensible and seek efficiency. "I think this value is in flux right now in the U.S. I think that the WWII generation more closely fit with imaginative and resourceful, but our society is shifting from makers to managers or services. In that sense efficiency gains and bottom line thinking is highly valued. I don't know if that is it truly emphasized or valued based on actions, but verbally it is all about the bottom line which I think accounts for a fair amount of the outsourcing trend in many industries."

Intuition

Americans may think of themselves as also having a few intuitive traits. The US is "very structured, but also built on resourceful, inventive and entrepreneurial people. Some of the US is theoretical and well-read (northeast) and some experiential." One East Coast American thought practical (sensing) represented the blue collar and conceptual (intuition) the white collar. Americans trust experience yet may have a hard time separating that from theories. "I doubt most Americans actually understand the difference. See any news report that starts with, 'According to a recent study,' as an example of how Americans don't successfully separate hard, empirical science from the theoretical and initial observations. My take is that we are more pseudo intellectual and more of an instant gratification culture. Therefore we are more results-oriented. We don't want to think too much, we just want some product or service right at this instant."

EUROPE

Netherlands is ESTJ:

Clear				Slight			Clear
I				▓	▓		E
N				▓			S
F				▓	▓		T
P				▓	▓		J

Dutch culture also is imaginative (N), original (N), empathic (F), and casual (P).

I found it surprising that the Dutch were ESTJ. Looking at the culture I guessed they were introverted and feeling which would make them similar to their Scandinavia neighbors who are ISFJ. The Dutch are a good example of a 'balanced' type—they don't clearly prefer any function. However, they reported themselves as ESTJ just like Americans and British. One example of like minds getting together is the Dutch-American Treaty which allows Americans to start a business in the Netherlands with very little requirements—a couple of commerce-oriented ESTJ cultures getting together.

The Dutch tend to associate with Scandinavia but in some ways they also resemble the USA. For example, they have a national health insurance plan for lower incomes (which the US doesn't have) but those earning over 30,000 EURO a year must get private health insurance just like Americans, and casual work agreements aren't covered by national health insurance.

The Dutch report a moderate preference for thinking but also the feeling aspects of empathy, tolerance and consensus can be seen in their culture. An example of empathy is their regard for the homeless. The Netherlands and the US are both extraverted thinking cultures but Americans don't have a feeling preference for empathy. The Dutch guru of culture Hofstede wrote in his book, *Masculinity and Femininity*, that the Dutch care for others and were shocked to hear American students say the homeless were no concern of theirs. Another example of Dutch empathy is they seek to understand others through the MBTI. 2004 was a big year for Dutch translations of the standard MBTI books. Logic is the opposite preference of the empathic Dutch. "Like their neighbors, the Dutch will also find themselves caught in the wage-leveling logic of globalization." (Jeff Gates, *The Ownership Solution*).

The Dutch also show their feeling preference with an open mind and tolerance for gays and drug use. "Another thing to be proud of is the Dutch being open minded. Amsterdam is the gay capital of Europe and every year the Amsterdam Gay Pride, a parade on ships on the Amsterdam canals, is being held. Gays are rather accepted by the Dutch than for example Muslims." Like Americans, Dutch claim to be tolerant but there seems to be a limit.

Feeling types value consensus. Americans believe in contracts but the Dutch believe in consensus. "The Dutch have long been methodical in their consensus building, proving themselves masterful at avoiding the ideological divides so common in Britain, France and now Germany. In essence, labor accepts a measure of financial discipline and business accepts a relatively pricey welfare state." (Jeff Gates, *The Ownership Solution*).

The Dutch have only a slight preference for sensing therefore also prefer some aspects of intuition. For example, the Dutch thought of imaginative and original "ways to deal with the water, since the Netherlands lay 1.5 meters below sea level and they have many canals, rivers and lakes, they invented floating bridges, which adjust to the level of water. Even floating houses are built and if you want to move to another region in the Netherlands, you just take your house with you."

Several Dutch disagree on whether they are introverted or extra-verted, although the majority picked extraversion. I wonder if there are regional differences? There doesn't appear to be many subcul-tures because the demographics of the Netherlands are: Dutch (80.9%), Indonesians, Surinamese, Moroccans, Turks and others (19.1%).

Most Dutch chose extraversion but Hofstede said the Dutch spend more time in introspection compared to Americans. They also show their introvert side by presenting themselves modestly. Newcomer to the Netherlands are encouraged to be modest, e.g. downplay personal abilities and achievements, don't show off wealth, etc. The Dutch as sensing and thinking types are efficient, pragmatic, believe concrete facts and empirical evidence over hypo-thetical, theoretical data or subjective feelings. Lastly, the Dutch report themselves as judging but also have a preference for being casual and easy going.

UK (England) is ESTJ:

Clear				Slight			Clear
I				▓			E
N				▓	▓		S
F				▓			T
P					▓	▓	J

English culture also is contained (I), quiet (I), accommodating (F), and tender (F).

The demographics of the UK are: English (81.5%), Scottish (9.6%), Irish (2.4%), Welsh (1.9%), Ulster (1.8%), Indian, Pakistani, and other (2.8%). The ENFP Irish are obviously very different from the ESTJ English. The Scottish and Welsh are also different but I was not able to persuade any of them to comment.

The English are the same type as the Americans, yet the English have only a slight preference for extraversion and thinking. Americans have a very clear preference for extraversion and thinking. Nevertheless, the English are extraverts. "They will be quite direct, ask questions, and will complain if necessary. Brits are good at joining things. People will always introduce each other at a social gatherings." The English differ from Americans because English are quiet and contained: "British stiff upper lip, don't make a fuss or draw attention to yourself."

The ESTJ Brits also differ from the ESTJ Yanks because they prefer tradition over being original. There is a traditional hierarchy of royalty, aristocracy and the working class. Brits are "not too good at change, if it's done like this we don't see why it should have to change."

The Britsh value traditions like the Ascot Races.

Brits are classic introverted sensing types. They "like facts about things", "tend to be quite rational about situations, down play. Discipline is important to us." Brits "like to make plans but not sure how focused we are on the future. The way we do it is best. We like to know what to do and when we're going to do it."

As ESTJs they are systematic thinking types and therefore value "process and logic". Extraverted thinkers have intellectual theories of how things ought to be. For example, in the USA and the UK, many people believe that the poor need to work harder and the rich shouldn't have to support them.

The thinking Brits also have an accommodating side and tend to be split between tough and tender. Brits are "very often the voice of reason, don't want to take sides, very principled, and fair-play is important." They "can be quite critical, although often quietly." They value harmony—or at least superficially. They are "not very confrontational, so tend not to look for arguments." This may be where they clash with Americans who can be more challenging than harmonious.

Austria is ESTJ:

Clear				Slight			Clear
I				▓			E
N				▓	▓		S
F				▓	▓	▓	T
P				▓			J

Austrian culture also is receiving (I), contained (I), theoretical (N), open-ended (P), and pressure-prompted (P).

Hungary is ESTJ:

Clear				Slight			Clear
I				▓			E
N				▓	▓		S
F				▓			T
P				▓			J

Hungarian culture also is intimate (I), traditional (S), empathic (F), compassionate (F), and pressure-prompted (P).

Hungary was one of the most confusing countries to verify their type. Several Hungarians reported many different types (INTJ, INFJ, ENFP, ESFP) but two agreed on ESTJ. Hungary "has been being a melting pot of nations, ancient tribes, conquerors, refugees, minorities, nomads, aggressors and so on, for centuries, mixing blood in all over Asia, Proche Orient and Europe." Ancient 'Huns' were nomads and immigrated from Central Asia.

"Hungarians are very resourceful and had to be in the communist years! Women are the tender type, men are the one ticked 'macho' society." According to one type expert, ESTJs can be macho traditionalists. As extraverted thinking types Hungarians are skeptical, "pessimistic, only believe what they see, unable to be spontaneous, don't like new factors when their plan is ready."

Hungarians as extraverts are easier to know and self-revealing. They also have a feeling side and can be personal (empathic). "It is very easy to make friends with my fellow Hungarians, for example there was a guy I used to translate for whenever he needed to visit his GP (General Practitioner). He told me his whole life story in a space of the first five minutes and explained his situation. He was very trusting and opened up easily. He wasn't in a very fortunate situation, staying in a hostel, but he was very open about it, showed me where he was staying and gave me his Hungarian address in case I am ever stuck and need help."

Slovenia is ESTJ:

Clear				Slight				Clear
I				▓				E
N				▓	▓	▓		S
F				▓	▓	▓		T
P				▓				J

Slovenian culture also is contained (I), abstract (N), and empathic (F).

"A variety of different nations, one way or another, had an influence on Slovenian people throughout our history. Nevertheless, our origin is a Slavic one, as our language and appearance, so in general we resemble other Central-European nations. Slovenia has friendly relations with all countries, including neighboring ones." One UH student from the capital city of Ljubljana thought, "All the neighboring Balkan states have the same mentality."

Croatia is ESTJ:

Clear				Slight				Clear
I				▓				E
N				▓	▓	▓		S
F				▓	▓	▓		T
P				▓				J

Croatian culture also is abstract (N), theoretical (N), accommodating (F), accepting (F), and pressure-prompted (P).

21

INTP—Introverted Thinking plus Extraverted Intuition

The next two chapters are about the introverted thinking mental process. INTPs and ISTPs prefer to use introverted thinking the majority of the time. Their second choice, in the case of the INTP would be extraverted intuition, and for the ISTP extraverted sensing. Both these introverted thinking types are concerned with principles like fair-mindedness.

INTPs use introverted thinking and have a secondary preference for extraverted intuition. We all use introverted thinking when we use inner principles and categories as guides to analyze and define the world. However, the INTP uses it more and is likely to be better at it than other types. Introverted thinking is what INTPs use in their inner, private world so it's difficult to observe in their actions or words. INTPs second preference is for extraverted intuition. Extraverted intuitive types explore new possibilities and form new ideas from the world around them. INTPs use extraverted intuition in the outer world and for interactions with others.

One INTP said, "INTJs don't care if anyone knows about their research but an INTP cares. We want to get the word out and get recognition. Research isn't worth anything if no one can understand it or doesn't know it's there." He also commented, "I don't think any countries could be INTP because a culture couldn't function if it was INTP."

Some individuals reported Saudi Arabia, Iceland, Argentina and Chile as INTP. Other people didn't verify this so either they were confused or there might be a subculture or region in those countries that is INTP. Looking at culture research on Saudi Arabia and after interviewing a few Saudis, there may be a possibility of an INTP culture or sub-culture in Saudi Arabia despite getting the majority reporting ENFP.

22

ISTP—Introverted Thinking plus Extraverted Sensing

ISTPs use introverted thinking and have a secondary preference for extraverted sensing. We all use introverted thinking when we use inner principles and categories as guides to analyze and define the world. However, the ISTP uses it more and is likely to be better at it than other types. Introverted thinking is what ISTPs use in their inner, private world so it's difficult to observe in their actions or words. ISTPs second preference is for extraverted sensing. Extraverted sensing types engage all five senses, spontaneously interact with the world and live fully in the moment. ISTPs use extraverted sensing in the outer world and for interactions with others.

EUROPE

Poland is ISTP:

Clear				Slight			Clear
I		▓	▓				E
N				▓			S
F				▓			T
P		▓	▓				J

Polish culture also is initiating (E), conceptual (N), theoretical (N), empathic (F), compassionate (F), and systematic (J). (The end of Chapter 2 has a decription of each facet.)

"Polish people get easily along with other Slavic nations, such as: Czech, Slovakian, Russian, Serbian, Croatian. I think the sense of humor, reaction to different situations, and the similarity in our languages make our nations feel closer and easy to understand." One Czech (Poland's neighbor to the south) person also reported ISTP for the Czech Republic.

23

Building on Giants

The beginning of each chapter has a general description and some personal observations and insights into each individual type. This is not a complete explanation of each type and other books need to be referenced for a deeper understanding of each of the sixteen types and the eight mental processes. The more you learn about the eight mental processes, the easier it will be to make your own observations in the countries you live in or travel through.

There are already several giants in the field of psychological type that have written in-depth on the sixteen types and the eight mental processes. None of these books are comprehensive and each carries different research and insight, therefore it's worth looking at them all.

If you would like to learn more about the basics of personality type please read:
- *Gifts Differing* (1980) by Isabel Briggs Myers (INFP). Myers is the creator of the Myers-Briggs Type Indicator (MBTI) instrument. Myers & McCaully (INFP) adapted Jung's work to author and refine the MBTI.
- *People Types & Tiger Stripes* (1979) by Gordon Lawrence. Lawrence (ENTP) explains it all: type dynamics, persona, shadow, etc.

- *Please Understand Me II* (1978) by David Keirsey (INTP). Keirsey adapted the work of Jung, Myers and others in this bestselling book.
- *Type Talk* (1988) by Otto Kroeger (ENFJ) & Janet Thuesen (INFP). This book is also a bestseller.
- *The Art of Speedreading People* (1998) by Paul D. Tieger (ENFP).
- *Building Blocks of Personality Type* (2006) by Leona Haas (ENFJ) and Mark Hunziker (INTJ). This is a good book for learning about the eight mental processes.

For even more depth (beyond the basics) on personality type I recommend the following:

- *Psychological Types* (1923) by Carl Jung (INTP). This cryptic and complex book is the foundation of the MBTI theory.
- *Was That Really Me?* (2002) by Naomi Quenk (INFP). Quenk builds on Jung's concept of the shadow personality.
- *Awakening the Heroes Within* (1991) by Carol Pearson (INFP). This isn't a book about personality type but builds on Jung's archetypes.
- *Dynamics of Personality Type* (1999) by Linda Berens (INTP). This booklet explains the eight mental processes.
- *Character of Organizations* (2000) by William Bridges (INTJ). Bridges determines the personality type of a company's corporate culture.

For more depth on type and culture I recommend:

- Raymond Moody's (INTJ) type & culture research and Psychological Type and Culture conferences in Hawaii.

Hofstede

Outside the world of personality type and in the world of business and industrial psychology there is the work of Geert Hofstede, the intercultural research giant from the Netherlands. His most popular book, *Culture's Consequences* (1980), is based on a foundation of cultural-anthropology, sociology, social psychology, cross-culture psychology, and intercultural studies. Hofstede defines several dimensions of culture (i.e. collectivism-individualism, power distance, uncertainty avoidance, and Confucian dynamism) but the one I find most intriguing is masculinity-femininity. Hofstede wrote in depth on this dimension in his book *Masculinity and Femininity: The Taboo Dimension of National Cultures* (1998).

Hofstede defines masculine and feminine as ego vs social goals. In a feminine values society the roles and behavior expectations for men and women are the same (e.g. modest, tender, etc). In a masculine values society, like the USA, the roles and behaviors are not the same. However, it is socially acceptable for a woman to compete with men and even act like a man. In a feminine values society certain roles and behaviors aren't limited to just one gender, both men and women are liberated. For example, it is okay for a man to stay at home and take care of the kids and to show his emotions.

Type is about mental processes. The Hofstede dimensions (individualism-collectivism, masculinity-femininity, etc.) are about values. Mental processes are biological—hard wired in our brains—and values are learned. Culture tells you which mental processes and which values are rewarded in society. The feeling mental process has tendency to have feminine values because many feminine values take people into consideration and feeling types consider people when making decision. An extraverted feeling type is concerned with the welfare of others and introverted feeling types are interested in humanitarian issues or practical service to others.

I am a huge fan of Hofstede's masculinity-femininity dimension because it measures one of the most important aspects of a culture: human considerations. His feminine values dimension correlates with the empathy facet of the feeling mental process. Feeling types favor values centered on empathy and human considerations over being objectively impersonal. For example, Hofstede found that feminine countries spend much more on developmental aid to foreign countries than masculines ones. This is an example of empathic behavior (empathy revolves around values and human considerations) which is a facet of the feeling type. There is a lesser correlation between feminine values and the feeling facets of accepting, accommodating and compassionate. Whereas, masculine countries tend to correlate with the critical facet of thinking and the traditional facet of sensing.

There are five facets for each mental process. The mental processes are far more complex and illuminate far more characteristics, traits and behaviors than is possible with Hofstede's dimensions. The thinking-feeling mental processes provide a picture immensely more detailed than Hofstede's masculine-feminine values. Therefore, a feminine country like the Netherlands can value empathy (one facet of feeling) yet prefer thinking because they still prefer four out of the five facets of thinking. Mental processes provide a more complex and complete understanding of culture.

ISFJ Japanese and Swedes

In Hofstede's research of 70 countries, Japan was the highest ranked as a masculine values country and Sweden was the highest ranked as a feminine values country. Both the Swedes and Japanese reported themselves as ISFJ, and the Swedes were even characterized as the Japanese of Europe. However, the Japanese reported themselves to have only a slight preference for feeling over thinking. Many masculine traits are associated with the thinking preference. Japan is a feeling type yet at the same time has masculine values.

Japanophile and MBTI type enthusiast Christopher E. West said it's like the ISFJs to try to hide their feeling preference. For the ISFJ there is an awkward balance between introverted sensing and extraverted feeling. Extraverted feeling is in the service of introverted sensing. The extraverted feeling preference may get buried underneath this dominant sensors sense of duty, tradition, and loyalty. West gave the example of ISFJs males joining the military to hide their extraverted feeling and show the world they are not sensitive. He said even the military in Japanese TV shows are ISFJ and have an awkward feeling side.

Another example is the Japanese philosophy that 'if you don't work, you don't eat'. This belief is sensible, matter-of-fact and realistic—all sensing traits. Also, the Japanese believe that the homeless have chosen their life on the streets. They turn their backs on the homeless despite being a feeling type culture.

Japanese masculine values are taken from historical precedents and reinforced in modern day Japanese culture by their preference for introverted sensing. Japanese have a masculine definition of male and female roles: women should stay at home, men should work, men shouldn't show emotion, and men should protect the women. For the Japanese, the inequality of men and women is their dominant sensing preference for being conventional and avoiding breaking with tradition. This takes precedence over their secondary feeling preference for being accommodating and accepting. As a result, the introverted sensing Japanese can sometimes resemble a masculine values or thinking type.

A Relative Comparison with Hofstede's Dimensions

Surprisingly, the thinking-feeling type scales correlate with more the individualism-collectivism dimension than the masculinity-femininity dimension. Here is the correlations between Hofstede's dimensions and the personality types of countries:

- A low IDV (Individualism-Collectivism) score correlates with EFP therefore collectivists are introverted feeling type countries.
- A high IDV score correlates with TJ therefore individualists are extraverted thinking type countries.
- A low MAS (Masculinity-Femininity) score correlates with ISFJ and ESFJ therefore feminine values are introverted sensing and extraverted feeling type countries.
- A high MAS score correlates with ISTJ and ESTJ therefore masculine values are introverted sensing and extraverted thinking type countries.
- A low PDI (Power Distance) score correlates with ISJ and ESJ or introverted sensing type countries.
- A high PDI score (means unequal distribution of power) correlates with ENP and ESP, the extraverted perceiving processes. These are extraverted intuition and extraverted sensing type countries.
- A low UAI score (Uncertainty Avoidance) correlates with judging (J) type countries.
- A high UAI score correlates with ENP and ESP, the extraverted perceiving processes. These are extraverted intuition and extraverted sensing type countries.
- LTO (Long Term Orientation) correlates with judging (J) type countries with FJ at the top. In Hofstede's LTO research there are very few ESP and ENP countries.

Archetypes

In addition to type and culture there is also archetypes and culture. Just like there are a dominant mental processes in a person or culture there are also dominant archetypes. The eight mental processes and archetypes are concepts developed by Swiss psychologist Carl Jung in his book *Psychological Types*.

Archetypes are reoccurring themes or stories in the history of humanity. Jung called them "primordial images...the heaped-up, or pooled, experiences of organic existence in general, a million times repeated, and condensed into types." A single individual or a whole society plays out these themes. Carol Pearson in her book *Awakening the Heroes Within* builds on Jung's archetypes. Although there are hundreds of archetypes she defined six important archetype pairs (i.e. innocent/orphan, warrior/caregiver, seeker/lover, destroyer/creator, ruler/magician, and sage/jester).

Carol Pearson defined the archetypal qualities of cultures: The warrior and seeker are the dominant archetypes in American culture. The US is a "Warrior/Seeker culture in which we are surrounded by self improvement schemes, all of which are designed to help us live up to some standard or other." She determined the sage as the dominant archetype in Eastern Buddhist culture; on the other hand, Western Christianity is a "Ruler/Magician religion." Additionally, the magician and jester archetypes are part of the African and American Indian cultures.

Archetypes play out in individual lives and cultures like dominant themes that come and go in a cyclical way. The German culture played out the dark side of the destroyer during WWII and rebirthed to a new country after the fall of the Berlin wall. Currently, France with its riots is also playing out the destroyer as one of its rising archetypes. The destroyer is a reoccurring archetype as seen in France's history of revolution.

The mental processes (mind) and the archetypes (soul) combine together to create our psyche (the human soul, mind, or spirit). Archetypes are on the soul level and partly unconscious. Archetypes map the story of the soul like the mental processes map the wiring of the brain. Soul is the source of our calling. Our calling is different from our type sweet spot. Type is how our brain is wired and hitting the type sweet spot is doing what we are wired for. Whereas, living out the story of our archetypes is following the calling of our soul.

The introverted mental processes provide the connection to our archetypes. The unconscious ability of 'psychic apprehension' taps into the archetype images of the soul and psyche. The introverted mental processes uncover universal truths through this unconscious soul connection. Jung states, unconscious archetypes have "universal validity and everlasting truth. Its truth, however, is so universal and symbolic, that it must first enter into the recognized and recognizable knowledge of the time, before it can become a practical truth of any real value to life."

According to Jung, archetypes originate from the collective unconscious—an unconscious shared by all of us. Jung also suggested that this is where God resides. Chris West suggested the collective unconscious is a river and certain personality types are like different boats. Certain boats flow over the river in similar places, therefore, generally have the same archetype experience. For example, France is an ENTJ and has a destroyer archetype rising and subsiding throughout its history. Maybe other NT countries share this same archetype experience. The USA is an ESTJ culture and has a distinct warrior archetype so other extroverted thinking type countries probably have a similar dominant warrior archetype occurring in their culture and history.

Lastly, repression of one side of our personality type leads to acting out our dark side, and so does repression of archetypes. Archetypes have a dark side that when repressed show itself in people and culture through immature, negative behaviors, or at worst, violence and war. Becoming conscious of and expressing our archetypes has a positive empowering effect. Learning your cultures archetypes and mental processes as well as your own archetypes and mental processes leads to a fuller understanding and expression of yourself and your gifts. Archetypes are similar to type in that you have to be true to your nature and according to Pearson, "there is no way to be happy except by living out your own deep great story."

Final Word

One Silicon Valley blogger from India believes that one day culture will reside in a museum and everyone will speak English and there will be a single world government. I don't think that is going to happen, but even if it did, there needs to be a lot of intercultural understanding first. I do believe type and culture (including archetype) can set us on the road to personal, domestic and international understanding.

Acknowledgments

I would like to say a big thank you to Drew Massey, Rheba Massey, Steve Dinkel, Mark Massey, and the rest of my family for their support and input; and Jerrilynn Lilyblade for her generosity in editing and formatting the manuscript. I would also like to thank Mark Van Noy, Praveen Moses, Fazal Lakhva, Charles Thangaraj, Henrik Forsling, Bruce Suehiro and Toru Takamiya for their comments; Paul Beisman and Tanya Marks for encouraging words; and Ray Moody, Bernie Ostrowski, Christopher West and the members of the Honolulu MBTI group. Finally, a sincere thanks to the over 400 people around the world who provided insight into their countries.

About the Author

Brent Massey is a full-time, professional, freelance writer. He lives in Hawaii and is also the author of *Culture Shock! Hawaii*. Brent isn't a stranger to crossing cultural boundaries. He spent three years studying, working and teaching in Japan, and is married to a Japanese woman. He loves being abroad and has traveled throughout Asia and Europe. Some of the countries he visited are Italy, Germany, France, Netherlands, Switzerland, Thailand, Singapore, Taiwan and Burma.

His studies reflect his deep interest in foreign culture and social research. Brent Massey has a post bachelors certificate in Asian Studies, and a Bachelor of Arts in Social Science. His research interests are comparative culture, Asian studies, modern/popular culture, and personality type theory. He has spent several years studying personality type theory and foreign cultures. He is a member of the Honolulu MBTI personality type group.

In 2003, he was awarded the prestigious Japanese government Monbusho scholarship for his research proposal on the personality types of Asian countries. *Where in the World Do I Belong??* is based on this award winning research proposal. Brent Massey is very excited and enthusiastic about *Where in the World Do I Belong??* because it will introduce a new way for people understand themselves and the world around them. *Where in the World Do I Belong??* has international and lasting appeal to readers everywhere.

He can be contacted at brentmassey@yahoo.com or brentmassey@brentmassey.com. He is interested in hearing from people from around the world and about their countries.

Index of Countries

Printed in the United States
132581LV00001B/107/P